JUDAISM

Michael Maher

Judaism

AN INTRODUCTION TO THE BELIEFS
AND PRACTICES OF THE JEWS

the columba press

First published in 2006 by
the columba press
55A Spruce Avenue, Stillorgan Industrial Park,
Blackrock, Co Dublin

Cover by Bill Bolger
Origination by The Columba Press
Printed in Ireland by ColourBooks Ltd, Dublin

ISBN 1 85607 553 2

This volume is a revised and expanded version of *An Giúdachas: Buneolas ar Chreidimh agus ar Chleachtais na nGiúdach* which was published by Foilseacháin Ábhair Spioradálta: Baile Átha Cliath, 2004.

Table of Contents

Introduction

This book had its origins in lectures I have given for a number of years at two Dublin Institutes, the Mater Dei Institute of Education and the Milltown Institute of Philosophy and Theology. My aim in these lectures has been to introduce students, mainly Roman Catholics, to the richness and variety of Jewish belief and practice, and to give them an understanding of Judaism as it has been lived over the centuries and as it is still experienced today. I have tried to make the students aware that Jewish writers and scholars down through the centuries since New Testament times have produced a vast body of religious literature, and have developed a rich pattern of rituals and observances that gives expression to the religious genius of the Jewish people, and that has shaped the Jewish way of life. I have attempted to give the students an appreciation of the values of a religious heritage other than their own, and I have tried to make them aware of the lively dialogue that is at present taking place between Jews and Christians in many areas of the world, a dialogue that is only part of the wider inter-religious discussions that are a feature of the modern religious scene.

In this book, with the same goals in mind, I hope to reach a wider audience and to provide those in the Christian community who may be interested in Judaism — the religion in which Christianity has its roots — with some information about the Jews, about their beliefs, their festivals, their rituals and their customs. It is my hope that the readers will come away with a more sensitive understanding of Jews, of their way of life, and of the values that have enabled them not only to survive but to manifest such vitality in spite of the victimisation and the persecution they have endured for nearly two thousand years.

Since the end of the Second World War two factors have brought about a dramatic change in the attitude of Christians to Jews and Judaism. Firstly, in the period since 1945 New

Testament scholars have become increasingly aware of the Jewishness of Jesus and of his earliest disciples. It follows that if we are to know Jesus and the early Christian movement we must know the Jewish community in which Jesus and his first followers had their roots.

Secondly, and more importantly, the gruesome horrors of the Holocaust forced Christians to acknowledge that there was something wrong with a Christianity that could allow the murder of six million Jews to take place in the Christian West. During the Second Vatican Council the assembled Fathers faced up to this issue, and in a document on 'The Relation of the Church to non-Christian Religions' which was entitled *Nostra Aetate* in Latin, they made a statement on Judaism and on the Church's relation to the Jews, a statement that was destined to make a lasting impact on Jewish-Christian relations not only in the Roman Catholic Church but also in many other Christian communities.

In 1985, on the occasion of the twentieth anniversary of the publication of *Nostra Aetate*, Pope John Paul II received a delegation from the American Jewish Committee. At that meeting a spokesperson for the Jewish delegates, in an address to the Pope, said: 'The adoption of the Vatican Declaration on Non-Christian Religions ... marked a decisive turning point in the nearly two-thousand-year encounter between the Catholic Church and the Jewish people'. In his reply Pope John Paul II said:

> ... the relationships between Jews and Christians have radically improved in these years [between the publication of *Nostra Aetate* and 1985]. Where there was ignorance and therefore prejudice and stereotypes, there is now growing mutual knowledge, appreciation and respect. There, is above all, love between us: that kind of love, I mean, which is for both of us a fundamental injunction of our religious traditions and which the New Testament received from the Old.

Since these words were spoken in 1985 the conversations between Jews and Christians have continued, with the result that the 'mutual knowledge, appreciation and respect' to which the

Pope referred have continued to grow. On a few occasions the dialogue between the members of the two faiths may have been tense, even acrimonious. But it has always been sincere and open, and therefore productive.

The leaders of the Roman Catholic Church have not been content to leave the dialogue to official Jewish and Christian representatives or to small groups of enthusiasts from the two faith communities. Already in 1974 the Vatican Document 'Guidelines on Religious Relations with the Jews' declared that

> … Christians must strive to acquire a better knowledge of the basic components of the religious tradition of Judaism; they must strive to learn by what essential traits the Jews define themselves in the light of their own religious experience.

Our goal in the present volume is to introduce our readers to the 'basic components' of the religious tradition of Judaism, and to help them to dispel the ignorance, to overcome the prejudice, and banish the stereotypes to which the Pope referred in the quotation given above.

Judaism is a very complex reality, and there are many expressions of the Jewish faith. Scholars often say that one cannot legitimately speak of 'Judaism' in the New Testament period. Since there were several different groups who had their own understanding of what being a Jew meant, one should speak of the 'Judaisms' of that period. The same is true in our day. There is no such thing as 'Judaism'. There are many types of Judaism. We have, for example, Orthodox Jews, Reform Jews, Conservative Jews, Reconstructionist Jews, Hasidic Jews, Secular Jews, and within each of these branches of Judaism there is a great variety of belief and observance. There is no singular authoritative religious institution that makes decisions for all forms of Judaism. Judaism does not speak with one voice. There may be a Chief Rabbi in a particular country or region, but he cannot claim to make pronouncements that will be regarded as binding by all the Jews within the area where he exercises his role. An official statement, written in 1993, on behalf of Reform Judaism in America included the following lines: 'One of the guiding principles of Reform Judaism is the autonomy of the individual. A Reform Jew has the right to decide whether to subscribe to this particular belief or that particular practice.' Not all branches of Judaism are as broadminded as the Reform Jews, but in general it can be said that under the umbrella of 'Judaism' there are many Judaisms, many expressions of Jewish faith, and many manifestations of Jewish commitment. Nevertheless, in spite of the divisions that are to be found within Judaism, all religious Jews give assent to a core of beliefs, and they observe, with greater or lesser fidelity, a number of ritual observances.

The task we have set ourselves in this work is to outline these central beliefs and observances. Since Jewish beliefs and practices are rooted in what Christians have traditionally called the Old Testament, and what is now often called the Hebrew Scriptures, we will begin with a brief outline of the history of Israel during the biblical period. In this outline the reader will encounter the patriarchs, lawgivers, historians, prophets, poets, visionaries, and wise teachers who in their different ways contributed to the development of Israel's religious thought. The reader will find terms like Torah, exodus, covenant, clean and unclean, redemption, messiah, all of which have profound meaning for Jews and Christians alike. This fleeting overview of the Old Testament will be followed by a summary account of Rabbinic Judaism, the Judaism that developed after the destruction of Jerusalem in 70 CE. This will lead on to a brief study of the Jewish community as it exists today, and to a discussion of some of the many branches that constitute modern Judaism. We will then present some basic information about the traditional literature that embodies the beliefs and practices, the laws and customs, the traditions and the lore that make Jews what they are. In the next section we will turn our attention to the theme of sacred time as we study the Jewish festivals and the sabbath. We will then focus on sacred space as we discuss the synagogue and its place in Jewish life. The two most important Jewish prayers, the Shema and the Eighteen Benedictions, prayers that are recited daily by all pious Jews, will then be the subject of discussion.

The dietary laws, that is, the laws that determine the foods that are permitted or forbidden to Jews, form the theme of our next section. We will then consider the many rituals that mark the life cycle of individual Jews. Our next chapter will present a very brief overview of the relations between Judaism and Christianity over the centuries, and this will be followed by a short account of the Holocaust. We will then give the book a local colouring by presenting a short summary of the story of the Jews in Ireland.

Over the past half-century nearly all the mainline Christian Churches have issued statements about their understanding of Jews and Judaism in the light of the Holocaust. From this vast body of documentation I have chosen to present some of the statements related to this matter that have been published by the Roman Catholic Church. These statements will show how one Church's teaching about Judaism has developed from the first tentative statement in 1964, to Pope John Paul II's unreserved confession of guilt in 2000. We will end with a glossary in which we will explain some of the terms that are commonly used to refer to different aspects of Jewish life.

In the body of the book when I use Hebrew words — like kosher, Shema, shofar, Yom Kippur etc — that have gained the right of citizenship in the English language because of their frequent use by English speakers, I write them in Roman characters. Other technical Hebrew words — like *siddur, Kol nidre, minyan* etc — that are frequently used by Jews, but not well known to others, these I have put in italics. When a reader finds himself or herself confused by such Hebrew terms I hope that the glossary will help her or him to find an explanation or clarification of the challenging word. I have replaced the traditional BC and AD with BCE (before the Common Era) and CE (Common Era) respectively. In doing so I am following a practice that has become commonplace among writers who address themselves to people who are involved in Jewish-Christian dialogue. Since this volume is addressed primarily to Christians who wish to get to know Judaism, I have on occasion referred to

New Testament texts that are clearly related to Jewish rituals or Jewish texts. In such cases, the Christian readers' familiarity with the New Testament may facilitate their entry into the thought patterns of the Jews, and will enable them to link their own religious experience with that of the Jewish faith community.

In this book I do not attempt to show how Christian theology and Christian liturgy have borrowed from Judaism, and this for two reasons. Firstly, my aim is to introduce readers to Judaism as it is understood and practised by Jews. My purpose is to draw attention to the richness and the beauty of Jewish faith and tradition as they have evolved over the millennia and as they are experienced by Jews today. Secondly, since Christians have often used the Old Testament and, to a lesser extent, Jewish beliefs and observances to prove the superiority of the Christian faith, I choose in the present work to address Judaism on its own terms and to avoid comparisons between the two faiths.

I have already published a book in Irish entitled *An Giúdachas: Buneolas ar Chreideamh agus ar Chleachtais na nGiúdach* (Foilseacháin Ábhair Spioradálta: Baile Átha Cliath, 2004). In preparing the present volume I have thoroughly revised, reorganised, and greatly expanded the material published in that Irish book.

I wish to express my thanks to Ms Judith Charry, a very committed member of the Dublin Jewish community, and one who is well versed in Jewish ritual and tradition, for reading my manuscript. I greatly appreciate the many helpful comments which she made on my work.

A word of thanks and appreciation is also due to Chief Rabbi Yaakov Pearlman who kindly gave permission to take photographs in the Terenure synagogue, to Mr Raphael Siev, curator of the Irish Jewish Museum, who graciously allowed us to photograph several of the exhibits in the museum, and to Ms Statia Davey who provided all the photographs used in this volume.

CHAPTER ONE

Historical Overview

ANCIENT ISRAEL

Judaism as we know it today is heir to the religion of the ancient Israelites, a religion that can be traced back to Abraham, and contemporary Jews see their story as being in unbroken continuity with the biblical story. In the Bible, the story of Abraham is preceded by an account of the creation of the world (Gen 1-3), and by a series of narratives involving the nations of the world (Gen 4-11). But in Abraham we encounter the father of the Hebrew people, the ancestor of all the Israelites. According to the Bible Abraham, whose homeland was in Mesopotamia (Gen 11:26-31), was commanded by God to leave his native land and set out for some unspecified country (12:1-3). The words 'you will be a blessing' (v 2) have been seen by Jews, the descendants of Abraham, as both a command and a promise. They are conscious that they have a mission to enrich the lives of many peoples through the ethical and moral message of the biblical writers. They have a duty to be 'a light to the nations' (Is 42:6). They are confident that they could fulfil this mission, because they had heard the reassuring promise 'I will bless you' (Gen 12:2).

Trusting in the God who had promised his blessing, Abraham obeyed the divine command, and eventually arrived in the land of Canaan (vv 4-6). An episode that was to be of great importance in the life of Abraham and in the lives of his descendants through countless generations is described in Gen 17:1-14:

1. ... the Lord appeared to Abram, and said to him, 'I am God Almighty: walk before me, and be blameless. And I will make my covenant between me and you ... 4. This is my covenant with you: you shall be the ancestor of a multitude of nations. ...7. I will establish my covenant between me and

you, and your offspring after you throughout their generations for an everlasting covenant, to be God to you and to
your offspring after you. And I will give to you, and to your
offspring after you, the land where you are now an alien, all
the land of Canaan, for a perpetual holding; and I will be
their God. ... 9. As for you, you shall keep my covenant, you
and your offspring after you throughout their generations.
This is my covenant, which you shall keep, between me and
you and every offspring after you: Every male among you
shall be circumcised. You shall circumcise the flesh of your
foreskins, and it shall be a sign of the covenant between me
and you. Throughout your generations every male among
you shall be circumcised when he is eight days old ... 14. Any
uncircumcised male who is not circumcised in the flesh of his
foreskin shall be cut off from his people ...'

In this short passage we encounter several themes that continue
to be of prime importance to the descendants of Abraham down
to this very day:

• Abraham's relation with God is due totally to God's initiative: 'The Lord appeared to Abram, and said ...'.
• God chose Abraham and his descendants from among all
  peoples. The Jews, descendants of Abraham, are the chosen
  people. He is their God.
• Abraham and, implicitly, his descendants are called to live
  blameless lives.
• God entered into a covenant with Abraham and his descendants.
• God promised to give the land of Canaan to Abraham and to
  his descendants. To this day the Jews have a special attachment to that land.
• Circumcision is the sign of the covenant. Throughout the
  generations Jews have considered circumcision as a religious
  rite that sets them apart as the people of God.

Scholars today admit that it is impossible to establish a precise
date for Abraham. But the findings of archaeology render a date
around 1800 BCE plausible.

Abraham Our Father

The Patriarchs Abraham, Isaac and Jacob, were the founding fathers of the people of Israel. From among those three, Abraham was singled out for special honour in Jewish tradition. According to Sirach 44:19 'no one has been found like him in glory'. The Bible portrays him as a man of faith (see Gen 15:1-6) and obedience (see Gen.12:1-4; 22:1-15), and he became known in Jewish lore as 'Abraham our Father'. He introduced the custom of circumcision (see Gen 17:9-14) which was to become the most characteristic observance of Judaism down through the centuries. To this day in the ritual for circumcision the boy who is being circumcised is said to 'enter into the covenant of Abraham our Father'.

According to rabbinic legend Abraham observed all the commandments, even though they were only revealed to Moses at a much later time. Some texts identify Mount Moriah, the mountain on which Abraham was ordered to sacrifice his son Isaac (see Gen 22:1-2), with the site of the Temple in Jerusalem (see 2 Chron 3:1), where sacrifices were offered on behalf of the people of Israel. A tradition which is repeated in many texts tells how Abraham was subjected to ten trials. He was, for example, thrown into burning furnace because he refused to worship idols; he was ordered to leave his homeland and go to a strange land (see Gen 12:1); he endured famine (see Gen 12:10); he was commanded to slay his only son (see Gen 22:1-2). Abraham survived all these trials that tested his faith in his God, and in doing so he became a model for all Jews who have to endure persecutions and trials that put their faith to the test.

Scattered through chapters 17-35 of Genesis we find information about Isaac, about his birth, his youth, his marriage, his sons, and his death. One of the stories in which Isaac was involved is recorded in Gen 22. This story, which tells of Abraham's readiness to sacrifice his son Isaac, and which is commonly referred to by the Jews as 'The Binding of Isaac', was destined to leave a permanent mark on Jewish spirituality. According to some versions of the Jewish tradition, not only was Abraham ready to offer his son, but Isaac also offered himself as a willing victim. Because of this readiness for sacrifice, Abraham and Isaac became models for all Jews who should be prepared to undergo martyrdom as a proof of their allegiance to their God.

At a solemn moment in the New Year Liturgy, Jews appeal to God to have mercy on them for the sake of the merits of the Binding of Isaac:

> Remember unto us, O Lord our God, the covenant, the mercy and the oath, which you swore to our ancestor (Abraham), upon Mount Moriah, and may the act of binding his son (Isaac) upon the altar be present before you; and as he suppressed his tenderness to perform your will with an upright heart, so we beseech you, let your tender mercy suppress your wrath; and in your great goodness avert the heat of your anger, from your people, your city, your land, and your inheritance.

Isaac is not given an important role in the biblical account of his people's history. Much more important was his son Jacob whose story is told in Gen 25:19-35:29. Jacob's name was changed to Israel, and from his twelve sons came the twelve tribes of Israel.

The story of Joseph (Gen 37-50) brings the twelve tribes to Egypt, and thus sets the scene for the story of the slavery in the land of the Pharaos and for the Exodus that brought that slavery to an end. Questions about the historicity of Joseph's rise to power in Egypt, and about the identity of the tribes that were enslaved in that country, are hotly disputed among the historians. But archaeological evidence shows that it is possible that groups of people from Palestine could have entered Egypt from about 1700 BCE onwards.

The twelve sons of Jacob and their families – now called 'the sons of Israel' (Exod 1:1) or 'the Israelites' (v 7) – were subjected to oppression in Egypt (vv 8-14). It is possible that the 'Pharaoh of the oppression' was Rameses II (1290-1224). Chapters 2-15 of Exodus tell how the Israelites, as a result of direct divine intervention on their behalf, succeeded in escaping from the land of their enslavement. The events narrated in these chapters cannot be verified by extra-biblical sources. But we do know from an ancient inscription that a people known as 'Israel' was already established in Canaan about the year 1220 BCE. We must keep in mind, however, that the author of these chapters in Exodus was

Jacob – Israel

In Jewish tradition, Jacob, who had his name changed to Israel (Gen 32:28), was seen as the representative of the people of Israel, while Esau with whom he had struggled in the womb (Gen 25:21-23), became the symbol of Israel's enemies. Jacob is therefore portrayed as virtuous, while Esau is seen as wicked. We are told, for example, that when the infants were in the womb, if their mother stood near synagogues or schools Jacob struggled to come out; if she passed near idolatrous temples Esau struggled to come out. Jacob, who dwelt in tents (Gen 25:27), was a studious man who frequented the academies; Esau, who was born red (25:25), was a shedder of blood. That is to say, the midrash took the image of Jacob living in tents to refer to Israel that was committed to the study of Torah, and it took the fact that Esau was born red to point to Rome, the kingdom that was continually engaged in war and bloodshed.

The fact that Jacob deceived Isaac in order to acquire the birthright (see Gen 27) created a moral problem for the rabbis. One solution was to claim that Jacob did not act from selfish motives. He knew that at that time, before the priesthood was established, it was the duty of the firstborn to offer sacrifices, and seeing that the wicked Esau was unworthy to perform such a function, he strove to get the birthright for himself. Elsewhere, Jacob's own piety is illustrated by the fact that it was he who introduced the custom of reciting the daily evening prayer.

Since Jacob was the ancestor of the Israelites, his trials and struggles, e.g. his wrestling with the angel (Gen 32:24-31), were seen as symbolic of the trials and persecutions the Israelites would have to endure in the course of their history. The traditional Passover Haggadah states that 'in every generation they rise against us and seek our destruction; but the Holy One, blessed be he, always rescues us from their hand'. The text then goes on to illustrate the truth of this statement by telling how Jacob was badly treated by Laban (see Gen 29-31), and how his immediate descendants were ill-treated in Egypt (see Exod 1-2). The lesson for the Jews is that just as Jacob and his family survived persecution, so will his descendants throughout the generations live on in spite of the oppression of hostile powers.

not primarily interested in writing a historical account. His main purpose was to make a theological statement about the origins of the people of Israel. For this author, God is the main actor in the story. It is God who enabled the Israelites to escape from Egypt and from the oppression of the mighty Pharaoh. This escape, which became known as the Exodus, is still celebrated by Jews as a key episode in the history of the chosen people.

If God was the liberator of the Israelites, Moses was his chosen instrument in bringing about the redemption. He was the one who received a personal call to lead God's people to freedom (Exod 3:1-12), and to him was revealed God's personal name, Yahweh (Exod 3:13-15). He was the one whom God would later appoint as the mediator of his covenant and his Torah to the chosen people (see Exod 19-24). The privileges of the covenant relationship, and the demands of the Law that was revealed to Moses, were to be the guiding principles of Israel's life throughout the whole of the people's existence. Moses was given the task of communicating to the people of Israel God's instruction concerning the construction of the Tabernacle, the place where God dwells with his people (Exod 25:1-31:18). It was to Moses also that God gave instructions concerning Israel's sacrificial system (Lev 1-7), and it was to him that the task of instituting the priesthood was given (Lev 8-9). To him also were communicated the rules concerning clean and unclean (Lev 11). When the people abandoned their faith in God and worshipped the Golden Calf it was Moses who prayed on their behalf and won the divine mercy for them (Exod 32:1-35; Ps 106:19-23). Moses enjoyed a privileged relationship with God, so that the Bible could say that the Lord 'used to speak to Moses face to face, as a man speaks to his friend' (Exod 33:11).

Having left Egypt the Israelites spent forty years wandering in the wilderness (cf e.g. Deut 2:7; 8:2) before they reached the land of Canaan, the Promised Land (see Exod 3:17; Deut 1:6-8; Gen 15:17-21). This probably took place toward the end of the thirteenth century BCE. The Book of Joshua continues the story of the conquest of the Canaanites and the settlement of the Israelites in Canaan. Joshua 24 describes how the Israelites entered into a solemn covenant, committing themselves to reject other gods, to serve Yahweh alone, and to observe the laws of

Moses Our Teacher

Moses, as portrayed in the Bible, enjoyed a privileged relationship with God, and he played a unique role in the Exodus and Sinai events that brought Israel as a people into being. The Lord, who 'used to speak to Moses face to face, as a man speaks to his friend' (Exod 33:11), made him the mediator of his covenant and of his Law to the chosen people (Exod 19-24). Nevertheless, Moses was never regarded as the founder of the Jewish religion. It was God himself who made a covenant with the people of Israel, and who gave them the Torah as their rule of life. Moses' role was that of an intermediary.

Still, Moses was given a prominent place in the lore and legends of Judaism. Sirach 44:23-45:1 declares that he (Moses) 'found favour in the sight of all and was beloved by God and people'. A little later on the same text states that God 'allowed him to hear his voice … and gave him the commandments face to face, the law of life and knowledge' (45:5). Since Moses saw God face to face, it is no wonder that he was considered the greatest of all the prophets. A passage in the Talmud says that although all the prophets saw God, they saw him as through a dim glass; Moses alone saw God through a clear glass. Because he had seen God, and because he communicated God's word to his people, the rabbis regarded him as the greatest of all Jewish teachers, and they usually referred to him as 'Moses our Teacher'. In using the term 'the seat of Moses' (Mt 23:2), Jesus was implicitly acknowledging the role of Moses as the supreme teacher of Israel. He was subscribing to the view that when the Scribes and the Pharisees taught in the synagogue they did not speak in their own name. They had to appeal to Moses as the source of their authority. Moses had received both the Written and the Oral Law on Mount Sinai, and any new interpretation or application of the Law which the rabbis might discover had been made known to him on the holy mountain.

Many legends illustrating the greatness and the virtue of Moses circulated in Judaism. It was said that when he was born the whole house was filled with light. When he was keeping his father-in-law's flocks (see Exod 3:1) he followed a kid that had wandered away. He followed the straying animal until it stopped to drink at a pool of water. Realising that the kid was thirsty Moses said 'you must be weary', and he put it on his shoulder and carried it back to the flock. Then God said to him 'since you showed mercy in leading an ordinary flock I will appoint you as leader of my flock Israel'. According to a tradition which occurs in the Talmud, Moses did not die but stands and ministers before God in heaven as he had done on Mount Sinai.

the covenant. We learn from the Book of Judges that in the period following their settlement in the land, the Israelites, who are now identified as a people (Judg 2:6-7; 14:3 etc.), were ruled by 'judges', charismatic individuals who led a tribe or groups of tribes.

The story of Samuel, the last of the judges (cf 1 Sam 7:6, 15), is told in the First Book of Samuel. Samuel was also called a prophet (cf e.g. 1 Sam 3:20) and, like the later prophets of Israel, he urged the Israelites to abandon false gods and to serve Yahweh with all their hearts (cf 1 Sam 7:3-4). Like other prophets who prayed for the people (cf e.g. Jer 7:16) he also made intercession on behalf of sinful Israel (1 Sam 7:5-6). It was he who anointed Saul as the first king of Israel (cf 1 Sam 8:1-10:16). This took place about 1020 BCE. Saul was killed at the battle of Mount Gelboa (cf 1 Sam 31:1-13) and the kingship passed to David.

At first David was anointed king of Judah (cf 2 Sam 2:1-4), and, at a later stage, he became king of Israel (5:1-5). David's reign began about 1000 BCE. He soon captured Jerusalem, established it as his royal capital and named it 'the city of David' (5:6-10). He received a promise from the Lord that his kingdom would never end (2 Sam 7:1-29; Ps 89:1-4, 19-37), and it was on this promise that Israel's hope of a future glorious Messiah was based. David is portrayed in the Bible as the ideal king who set the standard for all those who would later sit on his throne; see, e.g. 1 Kings 9:4; 11:4; 14:8; 15:3, 11; 2 Kings 14:3; 16:2; 18:3; 22:2. Nevertheless, the Bible does not portray him as flawless, and the biblical writer does not hesitate to tell the story of his shameful treatment of Bathsheba and her husband (2 Sam 11:1-12:25). It is interesting to note that when we first encounter David in the Bible he is introduced as a skillful musician (cf 1 Sam 16:14-23). It is to him that both Jewish and Christian tradition attributes the Psalms, Israel's treasury of religious songs and poems.

David's successor as king was his son Solomon (1 Kings 1:32-40). The new king, who took advantage of Israel's control of important trade routes, became very wealthy and was honoured by the leaders of the surrounding kingdoms (cf 10:1-29). His marriage to the daughter of the Pharaoh (cf 3:1-2) is proof that he was held in high esteem. His wealth allowed Solomon to engage in elaborate building projects, chief of which were the Temple in Jerusalem (5:1-6:38; 7:13-51) and a royal palace (7:1-12). Within the Temple, 'in the most holy place', Solomon placed the Ark of the Covenant (8:1-8) which contained the two tablets of the Law (v 9). Since the ark was a symbol of God's presence with his people, the Temple could be called a 'house for the name of the Lord, the God of Israel' (v 20; see Ps 27:4; 84:1-4), a place for him to dwell in forever (v 13). In this 'house of the Lord' (cf Ps 27:4) the people of Israel could rejoice, secure in the protection of their God (cf Ps 84:1-4). The Jerusalem Temple and its elaborate sacrificial system (cf e.g. Lev 1-9; 12-14; 16) were to become the focal point of the religious life of the people of Israel until its final destruction in 70 CE. However, during the early years of its existence the Jerusalem Temple was not the only place of legitimate sacrifice in Israel, and it was only about the year 621 BCE that King Josiah abolished all places of worship outside Jerusalem (cf Deut 12).

Solomon is famous not only for his wealth and for his building projects, but also for his wisdom which was manifested in many ways. His wisdom as a judge was acclaimed by all Israel (1 Kings 3:16-28), the vastness of his knowledge was proclaimed in the neighbouring lands (4:29-31; 10:1-10), and he is said to have composed 3000 proverbs and 1005 songs (4:32). Later tradition attributed the Song of Songs, Proverbs, Ecclesiastes and Wisdom to Solomon, although, as we now know, these books were written long after his time.

After the death of Solomon in 922, ten tribes broke with the Jerusalem king and appointed a king of their own. Now there were two kingdoms, a northern kingdom which became known as Israel and which consisted of ten tribes, and a southern kingdom which was called Judah. The Kingdom of Judah, which was made up of the tribes of Judah and Simeon, had Jerusalem as its capital. For some time different towns served as the capital of

Israel, but eventually Samaria became the permanent capital. The kings of the northern kingdom did little to promote the religion of Yahweh, and prophets like Elijah, Amos and Hosea, who preached there, strongly condemned their contemporaries for their wicked conduct and for their tendency to follow the religious practices of their pagan neighbours (cf e.g. 1 Kings 18; Amos 3:9-11; 4:1-3; Hos 4:1-14). When the Assyrians captured Samaria in 721 BCE, this disaster was seen as a punishment for the people's lack of allegiance to Yahweh and for their failure to observe his law (cf 2 Kings 17:5-23). With the fall of Samaria the Kingdom of Israel ceased to exist, and many of its leading citizens were taken into exile in Assyria and replaced by foreigners from different lands (vv 23-24). The new, mixed population practised a mixed religion (vv 25-41), and by doing so won the disapproval of the people of Judah. This marked the beginning of the hostility between the Jews and the Samaritans.

The Kingdom of Judah survived, but only because its king submitted to the Assyrians and paid tribute to them (cf 18:13-16). Even in Judah religious observance was lax, so that two kings, Hezekiah and Josiah, who were totally faithful to the religion of Yahweh, felt obliged to carry out religious reforms (cf 2 Kings 18:3-4; 22:3-23:25). During the reign of Josiah (640-609 BCE) the prophet Jeremiah also condemned the false religion of his contemporaries (cf Jer 7:1-34), while at the same time offering hope for the future (cf Jer 30:1-33:26). But by this time disaster threatened Judah from the East, and in 597 BCE Nebuchadnezzar, King of Babylon, conquered Jerusalem, and its king, with a large number of the leading citizens, were taken into exile in Babylon (2 Kings 24:1-4, 10-16). When the new king of Judah rebelled, Nebuchadnezzar attacked again. Jerusalem fell in 586. The account of the horrific burnings, destruction, plundering, execution and deportation that marked its fall is told in sober language in 2 King 25:8-21. The destruction of the Temple and the plundering of its treasures is told in prosaic terms (vv 13-17), although the tragic loss of this central monument of Israelite religion must have grieved the writer to the heart. With the fall of Jerusalem the monarchy and the Temple worship, the two great pillars of Israelite life, had come to an end, and the cream of Israel's population was in exile in Babylon. These unspeakable tragedies, which were mourned in moving poetry (cf e.g. Ps 137; Lam 1-5), remain etched in the Jewish memory to this day, and they are still commemorated on the ninth of Ab (July-August) each year.

Despite the shattering blow of 586, and in spite of the humiliation of the Exile, Israel survived, and in 539 Cyrus, King of the Persians, allowed the exiles to return home (cf Ezra 1:2-4). With the return there began a new and important stage in the history of the religion of Israel.

SECOND TEMPLE JUDAISM

The term 'Second Temple Judaism' is often used to refer to the Jewish religious system that developed in the period from the return from the Exile in Babylon (538 BCE) to the destruction of Jerusalem by the Romans in 70 CE. A key element in this religious system was the Jerusalem Temple that was rebuilt in the years 520-515 BCE. Hence the term 'Second Temple Judaism'. Cyrus, who set the exiles free, issued an edict which allowed the returnees to rebuild the Temple in Jerusalem at the expense of the Persians (Ezra 1:2-4; 6:3-5). The Jerusalem leaders did not allow the Samaritans to participate in the rebuilding (Ezra 4:1-3), and in doing so prepared the way for the hostility between Jews and Samaritans which is known to us from the New Testament (cf Lk 9:52-55; 10:30-37; 17:16; Jn 4).

After the return of the exiles, Judah became an independent Province within the Persian Empire and, according to Persian custom, the king acknowledged the local law as the law of the new Province. Ezra, a priest of illustrious ancestry (Ezra 7:1-5), and 'a scribe skilled in the Law (Torah) of Moses' (Ezra 7:6, 10-12), who had been appointed by the Persian king to administer the law in Judah (7:25-26), proclaimed the 'Law of Moses' in the presence of all the people (Neh 8:1-9). Thus the religious Law of the Jews became civil law, and the High Priest and the high-priestly families held religious and political power, subject, of course, to the over lordship of the Persians. The prophet Haggai, who wrote before the Temple was rebuilt, reflects the new political arrangement that formed the background to his work when he tells us that the word of the Lord was addressed to the 'governor of Judah', and to 'the high priest'. The High Priest was assisted by a council of 'elders' and priests (1 Macc 11:23; 14:20).

The social and religious atmosphere that prevailed in the new Province (Judah) was far from ideal. We learn from the prophet Haggai that economic hardship and scarcity were the lot of those who returned from the Exile (Hag 1:6-11; 2:15-19). The prophet Zechariah, who preached toward the end of the sixth century BCE, gives us a similar picture (Zech 8:10). Both Haggai and Zechariah proclaimed that the rebuilding of the Temple would bring divine blessings and the end of the people's misery (Hag 1:7, 9-10; 2:18-19; Zech 8:9-12). The books of Ezra and Nehemiah (written about 400 BCE) show that these two leaders had to condemn many abuses among the people. They outlawed mixed marriages (Ezra 9:1-4; 10:1-17), and they had to counter social inequality and oppression of the poor (Neh 5:1-19). Is 58:1-4, which was written shortly before the completion of the rebuilding of the Temple, reflects a situation in which injustice and oppression coexisted with external religious observance.

The establishment of the Persian rule in Judah marked the beginning of a 'new' Israel, an Israel in which Temple and Torah would be the most prominent features. So, for example, Pss 1, 19 and 119, which were probably written about 300 BCE, give expression to a piety that was centred on the Torah. The authors of 1-2 Chronicles, who wrote at about the same time, show that the Temple and its cult were of great importance to the writers. The Temple is the place where God's glory dwells (2 Chron 7:1-3), and the Levites render worthy service to the Lord (1 Chron 16:1-7, 37-43; 23-26). Divine favour can be won only by keeping the commandments (1 Chron 28:9; 2 Chron 15:2). Ben Sirach, who wrote about 200 BCE, identified Wisdom with the Torah (24:1-

29, esp v 23), and he showed great respect for the priesthood and for the Temple worship (Sirach 7:29-31; 50:1-21). But he asserted that sacrifice is an abomination if it is offered by one who ignores the rights of the poor (34:24-27; 35:1-9). Keeping the law and acting kindly towards one's neighbour is the best form of sacrifice.

The Hellenistic Era

The word 'Hellenistic' comes from the Greek word *hellenizo*, to imitate the Greeks, and ultimately from *Hellas*, which is the Greek word for 'Greece'. The Hellenistic period began when the Persian Empire collapsed before the onward march of Alexander the Great who, in the years following his accession to power in Macedonia, a territory just north of Greece, in 336 BCE, conquered most of the Mediterranean world, and extended his control as far East as India. At the death of Alexander in 323 BCE the Middle East fell into the hands of two of his generals, Seleucid who ruled in Syria, and Ptolemy who controlled Egypt. For some time Palestine was ruled by the Ptolemies, but in 198 BCE it came under the control of the Seleucids. By this time Greek culture was gaining a foothold in Palestine, but the Jews still retained a certain autonomy under their new rulers. They continued to be ruled by their own Law, the Torah, and the High Priest in Jerusalem ruled the territory. Under the Seleucid Antiochus Epiphanes IV, who came to power in 175 BCE, the situation changed. Jason, the brother of the ruling High Priest, bought the high priesthood from Antiochus and also received the right to establish Jerusalem as a Greek city. Having acquired those privileges Jason immediately set about hellenising the city (see 2 Macc 4:7-17). Three years later, however, a certain Menelaus, who had no qualifications for the high priesthood, approached Antiochus and outbid Jason for that honour (2 Macc 4:23-25). Having heard a rumour that Antiochus had been killed while on a military campaign in Egypt, Jason, in an attempt to regain the high priesthood, laid siege to Jerusalem. Antiochus saw this as a rebellion. He attacked Jerusalem, sacked the

Temple (2 Macc 5:1-23), outlawed the practice of Judaism, the observance of the Sabbath, the possession of copies of the Torah, and circumcision, and he set up a pagan altar, 'the abomination that makes desolate', in the Temple (1 Macc 1:10-15, 20-24, 41-61; 2 Macc 6:1-11; Dan 11:29-32).

Although many Jews were very willing to embrace Hellenism (1 Macc 1:10-15), there were others who resisted it, and this resistance became an open rebellion when the priest Mattathias refused to obey the king's command and called on others to join him (1 Macc 2:15-28). One of his sons, Judas, was nicknamed Maccabeus, 'the hammer'. Judas, continuing the revolt that had been initiated by his father, defeated the Seleucids, and, in the year 164 BCE, recaptured Jerusalem and rededicated the Temple which Antiochus had profaned (4:36-59). To this day Jews celebrate this event at the feast of Hanukkah. Eventually the Jews gained full independence, and the descendants of Judas Maccabeus, the Maccabees, held the reins of power. Having claimed royal status they became known as the Hasmoneans. They also took the position of High Priest (1 Macc 10:18-20; 13:36, 41-42), and the family that had gained prominence as opponents of Seleucid promoters of Hellenism, now became enthusiastic supporters of Greek culture.

At this time – in the second century BCE – various sects developed in Israel. The Sadducees were associated with the priestly families and with the ruling class in Jerusalem. They rejected the oral traditions and accepted only what is written in the Law. They did not believe in resurrection, or in angels and spirits. The Essenes are usually identified with the Qumran community. They probably originated as a group who opposed the Hasmoneans whose priesthood they regarded as illegitimate. They faithfully observed the Law according to their own strict interpretation. They believed that this observance, together with their life of prayer, substituted for the Temple worship, and made atonement for the invalid worship of the Hasmonean priests. The community lasted from the early Hasmonean period, about 150 BCE, until it was destroyed by the Romans in 68 CE.

The Pharisees adapted themselves to the situation under Hasmonean rule, and continued to promote the traditional religious practices. They were known as accurate interpreters of the Law, and they won the allegiance of the masses.

The Hasmonean kingdom came to an end when the Roman general Pompey took Jerusalem in 63 BCE. The Romans, having first appointed Herod the Great governor of Galilee, made him King of Judea where he ruled from 37-4 BCE. To win the favour of the Jews he rebuilt the Temple. The restored building, which was admired by Jesus and the disciples (see Mk 13:1-2), was a magnificent monument. The Jews resisted Roman rule and rebelled in 66 CE. But the rebels were defeated, and in 70 CE Jerusalem was captured and the Temple destroyed. A second Jewish revolt was crushed by the Romans in 135 CE, and from then on Jews were forbidden under pain of death to live in Jerusalem or even to visit it.

RABBINIC JUDAISM

Rabbinic Judaism, or forms of Judaism that stem from Rabbinic Judaism, will be the subject of the rest of this book. Here I simply wish to draw attention to some of the characteristic elements of Judaism as it was elaborated and formulated by the rabbis, leaving a fuller treatment of some of the topics touched on here to later in the book.

A key date in the development of Judaism was 70 CE, the year in which the Jerusalem Temple was destroyed by the Romans. Judaism of the pre-70 period is known to us from the New Testament and from other sources. It was a Judaism in which the Temple and its elaborate sacrificial system held a central place. The performance of the sacrificial ritual was purely a matter for the priests, and the lay people's role was that of passive observers. Pilgrims from all over the Jewish world converged on the Temple on the occasion of the great Jewish festivals (see Exod 23:14-17; Acts 2:1-11).

Judaism of the first century CE included several groups that were often antagonistic towards each other. Some of those groups,

The Diaspora

'Diaspora' is a Greek word meaning 'Dispersion'. It refers to colonies of Jews who live outside the Land of Israel. Ever since the deportation of the leading Jews to Babylon after the destruction of Jerusalem in 586 BCE, a large community of Jews flourished in Mesopotamia. After the conquest of the Middle East by Alexander the Great (c. 330 BCE), many Jews migrated to the west and settled in Egypt and elsewhere. There was a large colony of Jews in Alexandria, and by the first century CE there were Jewish communities in almost all the large cities of the Roman Empire. We know, for example, that there was a considerable Jewish settlement in Rome itself when Paul preached there. By the early second millennium Jews had settled in most European towns where they got involved in the money trade, so that they became identified with money and money lending in the Christian consciousness. From about 1820-1920, huge numbers of European Jews migrated to North America. It is estimated that between 1880 and 1920 nearly three million Eastern European Jews emigrated to the United States. Today the Jewish population of the United States is bordering on six million, about a million more than the population of Israel.

Down through the centuries the majority of Jews have lived outside the Holy Land, but Jews in every country remained strongly attached to the Land of Israel. The desire to return to the land that had been given to the Patriarchs was given expression in the following lines from the traditional daily Prayer Book:

Sound the great horn of our freedom; lift up the ensign to gather our exiles, and gather us from the four corners of the earth. Blessed are you, O Lord, who gathers the banished ones of your people Israel.

However, this prayer is little more than a pious formula for most Jews of the contemporary Diaspora. Jews everywhere ardently support the State of Israel, and many of them see the idea of returning to settle in the Holy Land as admirable and praiseworthy, but the vast majority of European and American Jews are content to live out their Judaism in the land of their birth.

such as the Pharisees, the Sadducees and the Scribes are known to us from the New Testament, while other documents reveal the existence of other groups. The Dead Sea Scrolls, for example, provide us with detailed information about the Qumran sect.

After the destruction of Jerusalem which brought the Temple worship to an end, the rabbis began to develop a Judaism that suited the changed circumstances. With Jerusalem out of bounds for Jews, a group of learned men assembled at Yavneh, about forty miles west of Jerusalem, for the purpose of establishing a form of Jewish life that could survive without Temple or sacrifice. In the period following the second Jewish revolt, known as the Bar Kochba revolt (132-135 CE), Yavneh was replaced by Usha, a town in Lower Galilee, as the centre of Jewish intellectual activity. Here the rabbis continued the task of interpreting Jewish law and formulating norms that would govern every aspect of Jewish life as it developed in new social, political and cultural circumstances. By 200 CE they had edited the Mishnah, a work that was destined to become the fundamental document of Rabbinic Judaism. The Judaism they taught became known as Rabbinic Judaism. Even today, all branches of religious Judaism appeal to the Mishnah, and they see themselves as ultimately derived from the Judaism of the rabbis. But it was not only in Palestine that the rabbis were engaged in intellectual activity. During the Bar Kochba revolt many scholars fled to Babylonia where they continued their Torah scholarship. In later centuries several flourishing academic centres developed in Babylonia.

A basic principle of the religious system of the rabbis was that God revealed a twofold Torah (the Hebrew word 'Torah' is usually translated as 'Law'), the written Torah, i.e. the scriptures, and the Oral Torah, i.e. laws which, according to rabbinic tradition, had been revealed at Sinai and handed on faithfully in an unbroken chain of tradition from the time of Moses to the days of the rabbis. The rabbis taught that 'Moses revealed 613 commandments: 365 prohibitions according to the number of days in a solar year, and 248 positive precepts corresponding to the parts of the human body'. It was these commandments, as interpreted and applied by the rabbis, that were to regulate every facet of Jewish life, religious and civil, for well over a thousand years.

The teaching of the rabbis was formulated and codified in the Mishnah, a collection of legal opinions that was written down about 200 CE. The Mishnah was studied, discussed and commented on by later rabbis whose views were put to writing in a body of literature that became known as the Talmud. We shall discuss both the Mishnah and the Talmud at a later stage. Suffice it for the moment to say that these two documents became the core texts, the foundation documents, of Rabbinic Judaism, and that they undergirded the legislation that was normative for practically the whole of Judaism from the sixth century to the nineteenth. Indeed, even the different branches of Judaism that have come into existence since the nineteenth century define themselves by referring to the laws and principles of the Mishnah and the Talmud. Some of those modern versions of Judaism affirm that those laws and principles must be followed to the letter, while others feel free to abandon some of them, and to reinterpret or adapt others.

Christians have often claimed that Judaism is a religion of legalism and external observance. It is true that traditional Jews have been, and still are, meticulous in their observance of the many regulations that govern their lives. But they observe these regulations in the spirit of the biblical precept which commanded them to love the Lord with all their heart and all their soul (see Deut 6:5). They regarded the Law as God's greatest gift to them, and as the clearest proof of his love for them, and they saw their own obedience to the Law as a proof of their love for God. They did not observe the Law out of fear or for the sake of a reward. A well-known text from the Mishnah reads: 'Be not like servants who serve the master in order to receive a reward, but be like servants who serve the master not in order to receive a reward'.

Worship, Prayer and Study

Although the synagogue existed before 70 CE, it was only after the destruction of the Temple in that year that it became the central institution of Judaism. Synagogal worship and prayer, which were complemented by a rich variety of home prayers

Rabbi

The word rabbi, 'my master', is derived from the Hebrew word 'rav', which means 'great, or 'distinguished'. It seems that the term Rabbi began to be used as a title for teachers and sages in Israel only in the first century CE. It must have been in current use with this technical meaning by the time gospels were written (see Mt 23:7). In the early Christian centuries the rabbi was one who had a profound knowledge of Israel's law, and who interpreted that law and applied it to the everyday lives of Jews. He could, for example, rule on points of ritual and on matters relating to the dietary laws. Since the rabbi received no salary, he practised some trade (doctor, shoemaker, trader etc) in order to earn a living. From the third century onwards some rabbis may have been paid by the community for their services as teachers. It was only in the Middle Ages that the rabbi, while continuing to act as official interpreter of the law, took on the role of spiritual leader of a Jewish congregation. But even then the rabbi did not regularly lead the congregation in prayer, and he did not officiate at marriages and funerals. It was only in the nineteenth century that these functions became part of the rabbi's duties.

The history of rabbinic ordination is not altogether clear. It seems that in the early centuries of the Common Era there were different degrees of ordination which commissioned different individuals for different functions, ranging from the lowest level of deciding only religious matters to the highest level of judging criminal cases. At one time individual rabbis could ordain those of their students whom they thought worthy of that honour. Later it seems that it was a court of rabbis who ordained. It is possible that at one time ordination was by the laying on of hands. But this rite was later abandoned, probably because it was adopted in the Christian rite of ordination. Nowadays rabbis are trained and ordained in rabbinic seminaries. In recent times, Reform, Conservative, and Reconstructionist Jews ordain women rabbis.

and rituals, have always had an important place in the Judaism of the rabbis. According to the Mishnah, a Jew was obliged to pray in the morning, in the afternoon and at sunset. The rabbis took the phrase 'to serve the Lord with all your heart' (Deut 11:13) to refer to prayer. However, study of Torah was considered more important than prayer.

The Sabbath, which begins at sundown on Friday evening, is

not only a day of rest but a day of prayer and study of the Torah. Observant Jews attend the synagogue services on Friday evening and on the Sabbath itself. Traditionally, Jewish men spend much time in the synagogue on the Sabbath studying and discussing religious matters. Daily prayers were said in the morning, afternoon and evening. The best known Jewish prayer is the Shema which is recited daily in the morning and in the evening. The great Festivals of the Jewish Year, e.g. Passover (Exod 12:1-13; Lev 23:4-8), the Feast of weeks, or Pentecost (Lev 23:15-22; Acts 2:1-11), Tabernacles (Lev 23:33-43; Jn 7:2), the Day of Atonement (Lev 23:26-32) are occasions of solemn liturgical ceremonies and communal celebration. The Seder meal at Passover is the high point of the Jewish year. It is a joyful celebration which takes place in Jewish homes, and it is an occasion when family members and friends rejoice together.

'And God Lamented'

According to an ancient tradition, although God decided to destroy the Temple because of Israel's sins, he later lamented when he saw the ruins of what had been his dwelling place among his people, and he mourned for his people who had been sent into exile:

At the time when God decided to destroy the Temple, he said, 'So long as I am in its midst, the nations of the world will not touch it; but I will close my eyes so as not to see it, and swear that I will not attach myself to it until the end [i.e. until the Messianic age]. Then the enemy came and destroyed it. ... They entered the Temple and burned it. When it was burnt, God said, 'I no longer have a dwelling-place in this land; I will withdraw my Shekinah from it and ascend to my former habitation.' ... At that time God wept and said, 'Woe is me! What have I done? I have caused my Shekinah to dwell below on earth for the sake of Israel; but now that they have sinned, I have returned to my former habitation. Far be it from me tha t I should become a laughing stock to the nations and a byword to human beings.' ... God said to the ministering angels, 'Come, let us go together and see what the enemy has done in my house.' ... When God saw the Temple, he said, 'Certainly this is my house and this is my resting-place into which enemies have come, and they have done whatever they wished.' At that time God wept and said, 'Woe is me for my house! My children, where are you? My priests, where are you? My friends, where are you? What shall I do with you, seeing that I warned you but you did not repent?' [God then summoned Moses and the Patriarchs to come and see the ruined Temple.] They immediately also rent their garments, placed their hands upon their heads, and cried out and wept until they arrived at the gates of the Temple. ... They went weeping from one gate to another like a man whose dead is lying before him. And God lamented.

CHAPTER TWO

Different Branches within Judaism

REFORM JUDAISM

Until about 1800 the Jews of Europe, who lived in segregated communities, had followed a pattern of believing and living that had developed during the Middle Ages. Until that date one could say that European Jews constituted a monolithic faith community that was governed by Jewish law as interpreted by the rabbis. But after 1800, due to the Enlightenment and to contact with modern culture, and a result of the emancipation of the Jews in the nineteenth century, many educated Jews in Germany were calling for changes that would bring Jewish religious practice and many aspects of the Jewish lifestyle into conformity with the demands of the modern world. These promoters of change and their followers developed a form of Jewish life that has become known as Reform Judaism. The Reformers made a distinction between elements of the Torah that are eternal, and legal customs that developed over the centuries in response to new situations. They regarded many of the dietary laws as outmoded and as no longer binding. They relaxed the laws governing the Sabbath. They abandoned belief in a personal Messiah who would lead the Jews back to Israel, and they gave up the hope of rebuilding the Jerusalem Temple and of restoring its cult. They attributed greater importance to the ethical and social teaching of the prophets than to ritual observances. In the liturgy they introduced German instead of Hebrew in some parts of the synagogue service; they shortened part of the service; they allowed sermons to be preached in German; they permitted organ accompaniment in the synagogue, something that had been forbidden by the rabbis. They established seminaries where rabbis would be trained according to modern scholarly methods.

Reform Jews accept the principle of gender equality, and in 1972 the first woman rabbi was ordained at the rabbinic College of the Reform Movement in Cincinnati, Ohio. Reform communities now celebrate *bat mitzvah*, the ritual that marks a girl's reaching the age of maturity. They proclaim the rights of homosexuals and lesbians, including their right to ordination as rabbis. In 1983 Reform Judaism adopted the principle of patrilinear descent, that is to say, they recognise as Jewish anyone whose father is Jewish, even though the mother may be non-Jewish. Until then only one who was born of a Jewish mother was automatically considered a Jew. Within Reform Judaism there is a great variety of belief and practice. People of radical and conservative views can enjoy membership of the same community.

The Reform movement had only modest success in Germany, but from about 1850 onwards it flourished in America. In the United Kingdom, Liberal Judaism corresponds very closely to American Reform. In Israel, Reform Judaism is known as Progressive Judaism. Although exact numbers are hard to calculate, a survey in 2001 led to the conclusion that there are about 1,100,000 Reform Jews in the United States. This represents 38% of American Jews who are affiliated to a synagogue.

In 1999, after considerable controversy, the Central Conference of American Rabbis, the authoritative body within Reform Judaism, agreed on 'A Statement of Principles for Reform Judaism' from which we take the following lines:

... We affirm that Torah is the foundation of Jewish life.

We cherish the truths revealed in Torah, God's ongoing revelation to our people and the record of our people's ongoing relationship with God ...

We are committed to the ongoing study of the whole array of *mitzvot* (commandments) and to the fulfilment of those that address us as individuals and as a community. Some of these *mitzvot*, sacred obligations, have long been observed by Reform Jews; others, both ancient and modern, demand renewed attention as the result of the unique context of our own times.

We bring Torah into the world when we seek to sanctify the times and places of our lives through regular home and congregational observance. ...

We bring Torah into the world when we strive to fulfil the highest ethical mandates in our relationships with others and with all of God's creation. Partners with God in *tikkun olam*, repairing the world, we are called to help bring nearer the messianic age. We seek dialogue and joint action with people of other faiths in the hope that together we can bring peace, freedom and justice to our world ....

ORTHODOX JUDAISM

Among those Jews who refused to follow the Reformers in nineteenth century Germany there was a group who became known as Orthodox Jews. The term 'Orthodox' is borrowed from Christian usage, and had not been applied within Judaism before the time of the Reformers. It was then used by progressive Jews as a derogatory term for those Jews who refused to accept the tenets of the reformers.

The Orthodox regard both the Written Torah and the Oral Torah as having been revealed by God to Moses at Mount Sinai. Consequently they say that the law is eternally valid and unchangeable. It cannot be modified or adapted in order to suit the values of a particular age. Orthodox Jews faithfully observe the traditional Jewish laws and rituals, and they see themselves as the only group who practise Judaism faithfully. They celebrate the traditional liturgy; men and women sit apart in the synagogue; there are no Orthodox women rabbis. Orthodox Jews only recognise as a Jew someone who was born of a Jewish mother, or who has converted to Judaism in accordance with Jewish law and tradition. The fact that the Orthodox refuse to recognise the marriages, the divorces and the conversions that are carried out by the rabbis of other branches of Judaism often brings them into conflict with other Jews.

Within the wider Orthodox community there is great variety. Indeed, people sometimes make a distinction between the

Modern Orthodox, or Neo-Orthodoxy, and the Orthodox, or ultra-Orthodox. The ultra-Orthodox, if we wish to use the term, are more strict than others in their observance of the halakah, and they show little interest in secular culture. Some of them refuse to acknowledge the State of Israel, since they believe that only the Messiah can establish a Jewish state. The more moderate wing of the Orthodox take a positive view of modern culture and scientific developments, and they believe that one can combine observance of the halakah with full involvement in modern life. The motto 'Torah and Civilisation' which they sometimes use expresses this point of view. In order to put this motto into practice they tend to be lenient in their interpretation of the halakah. They receive a sound secular education, as well as a solid religious formation, and they attend universities and seek middle-class careers.

The ultra-Orthodox continue to dress like their Eastern European forbears. Men wear beards and side locks, and black coats, white shirts and black hats. Women avoid the use of trousers and wear very modest dresses. Married women cover their heads with a wig or headscarf. Modern Orthodox Jews follow more or less the same dress codes as liberal and secular Jews. Men, of course, always wear a skullcap or other head covering.

An important group within the ultra-Orthodox movement are the Hasidim. This term is derived from the Hebrew *hesed*, 'good deed', and the hasidim are those who show a great interest in mysticism and personal spirituality.

Orthodox Jews are a minority within the total Jewish community. According to surveys carried out in the 1990s there are about 400,000 Orthodox Jews in America out of a total Jewish population of about 5,800,000. Of the 4,600,000 Jews living in Israel, more than 20% would identify themselves as Orthodox. There are about another 500,000 Orthodox Jews living in such countries as Britain, France, Belgium and Australia.

CONSERVATIVE JUDAISM

Like the Reform Movement, Conservative Judaism has its roots in Germany in the nineteenth century. The name 'Conservative' comes from the fact that the leaders of the movement tried to conserve the traditional Jewish way of life in the modern world. The promoters of the movement wished to steer a middle course between the Reformers and the Orthodox. They wanted to embrace modern scientific and cultural developments while remaining faithful to the spirit of the Torah and the rabbinic traditions. Today's Conservatives profess loyalty to the traditional Jewish legal tradition, while asserting the rights of their rabbinical authorities to interpret and to apply Jewish law in the light of the changing circumstances of our time.

The man who began the process that was to lead to the establishment of Conservative Judaism was Zacharias Frankel (1801-1875), head of the Rabbinical Seminary in Breslau, the first modern rabbinic school in Central Europe. Frankel caused an outcry among the Orthodox by publishing works in which he argued that the Oral Torah had not been revealed at Sinai, but had been a product of rabbinic thought. He and his followers began to study Jewish texts in their historical context and to apply the method of critical research to them. It is not surprising then that Frankel's school of thought became known as the 'Historical School', or the 'Historical Movement'. Its proponents showed that although the essentials of Judaism have always remained, some aspects of Jewish life have been modified down through the centuries. It is the task of scholarship to establish what elements were considered essential for the Jewish way of life in the early centuries of Judaism. These same elements must be considered essential today, and other elements may be discarded or modified. Following these principles, the Historical Movement could claim that its aim was to conserve the ancient faith of Judaism, and to abandon the accretions of later centuries, accretions which, according to the followers of that Movement, are of little or no relevance in the modern world.

In the United States the principles of the Historical

Movement became the basis for Conservative Judaism, which has as its motto the words 'Tradition and Change'. This motto indicates that while the Conservatives value and cherish tradition, they also believe that traditional laws and traditional understandings of sacred Jewish texts can be modified when circumstances demand this. Since Conservative Judaism leaves considerable freedom to individual congregations, practices vary from synagogue to synagogue. In principle, Conservative Jews observe the traditional halakah and the traditional rituals. So, for example, a Conservative Jew is expected to observe the Sabbath faithfully and to keep kosher. But in practice Conservative Jews do not always follow a rigid interpretation of the laws of Sabbath or kosher. So, for example, people are allowed to drive to the synagogue on the Sabbath for the purpose of attending worship, although driving on the Sabbath was strictly forbidden by traditional law. A Conservative Jew may turn on or off certain electrical appliances, such as lights, radio, television, a microwave for the purpose of heating cooked food etc. According to a survey carried out in 1990, only 24% of Conservative families observe kosher.

Men and women play equal roles in the Conservative community. In 1985 the first Conservative woman rabbi was ordained. In most Conservative synagogues women may be called to read the Torah in the synagogue, and they may be counted in the *minyan*.

Statistics resulting from a survey that was carried out in the mid 1990s indicate that Conservative Jews then formed about 36% of the American Jewish community. There are also thriving communities of Conservative Jews Canada, as well as smaller communities in Israel and Beunos Aires.

The following excerpt from a 'Statement of Principles of Conservative Judaism', which was published in 1988, helps us to understand how the Conservatives see themselves:

... Since each age requires new interpretations and applications of the received norms, Halakah is an ongoing process.

... We in the Conservative community are committed to carrying on the rabbinic tradition of preserving and enhancing Halakah by making appropriate changes in it through rabbinic decision. ... The rapid technological and social changes of our time, as well as new ethical insights and goals, have required new interpretations and applications of Halakah to keep it vital for our lives; more adjustments will undoubtedly be necessary in the future. These include additions to the received tradition to deal with new circumstances, and in some cases, modifications of the corpus of Halakah.

RECONSTRUCTIONIST JEWS

The branches of Judaism which we have just considered – Reform, Orthodox, Conservative – had their beginnings in Germany. Reconstructionism, however, is a purely American creation. Its founder, Rabbi Mordechai Kaplan (1881-1983), who was the son of an Orthodox rabbi, arrived in America from Lithuania at the age of nine. Given this fact, it is not surprising that his early education was Orthodox and traditional. Nevertheless, he was ordained a rabbi at the Jewish Theological Seminary, New York, which is the rabbinic seminary of the Conservative Movement. He served as Rabbi in an Orthodox community, and taught at the Jewish Theological Seminary. He founded the Society for the Advancement of Judaism in 1922, and the Jewish Reconstructionist Federation in 1955.

Kaplan and his followers, the Reconstructionists, saw Judaism not just as a religion, but as an 'evolving religious civilisation'. This civilisation consists of the history, the language, the culture and customs of the Jewish people, and the people's attachment to the Land of Israel. The Reconstructionists deny the existence of a personal, transcendent God who intervenes in human affairs. Their God is a God who dwells in our world, and especially in the human heart. They reject the belief that the Torah was revealed at Sinai. Jewish beliefs, laws and practices are, they say, the result of continuous growth and development over the centuries. Furthermore, each generation must continue the process of change and development. The Reconstructionists believe that the ability to change and adapt allows Judaism to continue as a dynamic tradition in every age.

Although the Reconstructionists do not regard the classical texts of traditional Judaism as the revealed words of God, they continue to study them because they express the culture, values and insights of the Jewish people. They value traditional obser-vances, such as the Sabbath and the kosher regulations, not as something that has been commanded by God, but as treasured reminders of the people's past. They see the synagogue not solely as a place of worship and prayer, but as a Jewish community centre, where all kinds of Jewish social and cultural activities may take place. The movement does not regard the Jews as a specially chosen people, but regards all people as bearers of the divine image and capable of developing an intimate relationship with God. Reconstructionism is the most democratic of the branches of Judaism, in the sense that important decisions that affect the community are reached through reflection and discus-sion by members of the community and the rabbi.

SECULAR JEWS

Before the Jewish thinkers and writers came under the influence of the Enlightenment in the late eighteenth and nineteenth cent-uries, the Jews were not troubled by questions about their iden-tity. They would have readily subscribed to the words of Ruth, the Moabite, who, on the occasion of her conversion to the faith of Israel, declared: 'Your people shall be my people, and your God my God. Where you die, I will die' (Ruth 1:16-17). The key elements in this statement are a shared faith and a shared fate. And the two elements were inextricably linked. Religion and peoplehood went together. This, however, is no longer true. Today one can be a Jew without professing any religious alleg-iance. By the end of the nineteenth century the religious authori-ties had lost much of their traditional control over the Jewish community, and members of that community could abandon all religious observance without fear of censure. By then many of those who promoted Zionism, a movement that was to have far-reaching effects on Judaism, would have understood Judaism in purely secular terms. They would have defined it in terms of people, land, language and culture.

Nowadays, Jews who have turned their backs on religion can rightfully claim full membership of the Jewish people. To claim Jewish identity does not imply acceptance of Jewish religious belief. One can assert one's Jewishness but reject Judaism. Even the Orthodox community has come to recognise as Jewish any-one born of a Jewish mother, even though that person may be completely non-religious. Since 1983, Reform Jews recognise as Jewish anyone born of either a Jewish father or a Jewish mother. For Jews who have no religious allegiance, Judaism is a matter of ethnic, historical, cultural or national identity, and it owes lit-tle or nothing to inherited religious convictions. Such terms as Torah, Passover, Covenant and Messiah etc have lost their reli-gious meaning for secular Jews and for many liberals. The Passover Seder, for example, is regarded as a 'cultural' or social event, rather than as a religious and spiritual experience. It is in and through cultural and social events, and not through reli-gious belief, that many modern Jews experience and express their Jewish identity.

KABBALAH AND HASIDISM

Neither Kabbalah nor Hasidism can be regarded as a branch of Judaism in the same way as the groupings we have just been considering. Nevertheless, since they are movements that have had a long history in Judaism and an enormous influence on Jewish piety, we give them a place in the present chapter.

Kabbalah

The basic meaning of the Hebrew word *kabbalah* is 'tradition'. But ever since the eleventh century, when the term 'kabbalah' was first applied by Spanish writers to Jewish mysticism, the term has been taken to refer to Jewish mystical teachings. It con-sists largely in an interpretation of the Bible that attempts to dis-cover the deepest, concealed meaning of the words and letters. Elements of mystical speculation are found in the Talmud and

Midrash, and this mystical tradition appeared in a developed form by the sixth century CE. A few books that may have been composed before 600 CE, claim to show how one can reach communion with God through study of the letters of the Hebrew alphabet, and through the use of magical names and formulae.

These early works were highly obscure and enigmatic, but they did influence the Kabbalistic Movement proper which developed between the twelfth and the fourteenth centuries in southern France and Spain. Independently of this movement, different schools of mysticism developed in the Rhineland and in Northern France in the twelfth and thirteenth centuries. The leaders of these Spanish, German and French schools produced a rich literature, developed a variety of esoteric theologies, and taught different forms of piety and asceticism that would enable the soul to acquire a deeper understanding of the Torah and a closer relationship with God. The German school in particular promoted very severe ascetical exercises, including self-flagell-ation.

In the fourteenth and fifteenth centuries kabbalistic schools appeared in Italy, Greece and Israel. In Safed, in Northern Galilee, Isaac Luria (1534-1570) developed a new form of kabbal-ah, one that was strongly messianic in character. According to this new kabbalah, every Jew has a part to play in the work of re-pairing or restoring our broken world, and of ridding it of evil and impurity. Through fidelity to the ritual observances, through prayer, ascetical exercises, and through the observance of the *mitzvot*, the Jew helps to counteract the evil that is around us, and in doing so prepares the world for the coming of the Messiah. The proponents of this doctrine were convinced that the process of repairing was almost complete, and that the final redemption would soon be a reality. The responsibility of com-pleting the process rests upon Israel as a whole. If one Jew fails to make a contribution to the task, others must bear the extra burden. It is easy to understand how this teaching would prove attractive to persecuted Jews everywhere.

One of those who was strongly influenced by the kabbalistic

teaching of Luria was Shabbetai Tzvi (1626-1676). Born in Turkey, he received a thorough Talmudic education, and he also became proficient in kabbalistic lore. For some years he lived in semi-seclusion and followed an ascetic way of life. Scholars today believe that he was a manic depressive. Having lived for some time in Greece, Jerusalem, Cairo and Gaza, he proclaimed himself Messiah in 1665. The announcement created a frenzy of excitement among the Jewish communities, and the newly pro- claimed Messiah soon had large numbers of enthusiastic follow- ers not only in Palestine and Turkey but also in North Africa and all over Europe. Convinced that the Sultan of Turkey would ac- cept his messianic claims and surrender his throne to him, Shabbetai set out for Constantinople. But when, accompanied by many followers, he arrived there in 1666 he was effectively put under house arrest. The Sultan listened to his proposal, but after some debate with his court, he presented Shabbetai with the choice of death or conversion to Islam. The would-be Messiah accepted the latter choice. His apostasy left many of his followers in a state of shock and confusion, and there were those who concluded that Shabbetai's kabbalistic views were the cause of the whole disaster. As a result kabbalah fell into dis- favour in some places, and some brilliant kabbalists became vic- tims of harsh condemnation and persecution.

Until the sixteenth century kabbalah was the preserve of esoteric circles. Throughout the seventeenth and eighteenth centuries, however, Judaism as a whole was heavily influenced by kabbalistic ideas. Kabbalah was a major influence in the de- velopment of Hasidism, and Hasidic Judaism has in turn been a powerful vehicle for the spread of kabbalah in modern times.

The Zohar, a book of Jewish mystical teaching that was writ- ten in Spain in the second half of the thirteenth century, became the greatest classic of Jewish mysticism. It became very popular among the Hasidim, the revivalist movement that had it origins in Poland in the eighteenth century. Written in Aramaic – in order to give the impression that it was an ancient text – the Zohar is largely a mystical commentary on the Torah. It contains esoteric discussions on such topics as the nature of God, the origin of the world, good and evil. Besides the Zohar, Jewish kabbalah has produced a vast body of literature that is practically inaccessible to the uninitiated. Without some knowledge of Hebrew, and without a reasonable familiarity with the Bible and the Talmud, one cannot understand or appreciate Jewish kabbalah. Those who have seriously studied kabbalah and understand it, look askance at some recent centres for kabbalistic teaching that are proving attractive to a number of celebrities. Some of those popular centres, the scholars say, are not teaching genuine Jewish kabbalah, but a pop-psychology version of kabbalah. They are responding to people who are in search of quick-fix solutions for personal problems, and they are dishing out new-age teachings dressed up in the language of kabbalah.

Hasidism

The Hebrew word *hasid* (plur *hasidim*) means 'pious'. The term *hasidim*, 'pious ones', is now used to refer to members of the revivalist movement, Hasidism, that originated in south-eastern Poland in the eighteenth century. The Hebrew word *hasid* is derived from the word *hesed*, 'good deed', and the hasidim believed that it is through good deeds and prayer that one gains intimacy with God. They regarded religious emotions as more important than academic religious knowledge. They could therefore be seen as challenging the position of the rabbis who claimed that it was only through rigorous and disciplined study that one acquires holiness. The Hasidim were also providing an alternative to the complex mystical religion of the kabbalah.

In the 1730s, without wishing to break with either rabbinic tradition or with kabbalah, the Hasidim rallied round a charismatic individual whose real name was Israel ben Eliezer, but who was to become popularly known as the Baal Shem Tov (c. 1700-1760), 'Master of the Good Name'. This popular teacher, who had already achieved a reputation as a healer, now created a new form of mysticism by combining rabbinic religion with kabbalistic doctrines. He insisted that God is present everywhere, and that he can be served, not only when one obeys the Torah, but in all that one does. One is close to God in such ordinary activities as eating, drinking, doing business and enjoying sex. God himself is present in a person's troubles, spiritual and physical. The Baal Shem Tov wished to bring a note of joy, warmth and exuberance into Jewish worship and spirituality, which in Poland had become too formal, largely divorced from the harsh realities of contemporary Jewish life, and therefore unable to satisfy the religious needs of the Jewish masses. The Baal Shem Tov taught that true religion is not a matter of rabbinic learning, but of sincere love of God and prayer. He communicated his message not through formal lectures, but in sayings and parables. His successors taught that only a few people can become a *tsaddiq*, that is, a truly devout and learned person who has achieved intimacy with God. It is through following the guidance of such a *tsaddiq* – or Rebbe, as these spiritual leaders were known in hasidic communities – that other people reach God. This new brand of Jewish spirituality spread quickly throughout Poland, and by the 1770s it was being severely condemned by the leading rabbis of the day who saw their authority being challenged by this populist movement. But the new movement continued to expand, and by the eighteenth century it was well established in practically the whole of Eastern Europe. It dominated Jewish religious life there throughout the nineteenth century.

In the early 1880s, as a result of the pogroms in Russia and Poland, there were massive emigrations from the centres of Hasidic Judaism. The emigrants settled especially in the United States and in Israel. The Holocaust wiped out the hasidic centres of Europe, and the survivors emigrated to Israel and to the United States, especially to New York, and today these are the main centres of Hasidic Judaism.

Ashkenazi Jews

The Hebrew personal name Ashkenaz occurs in Gen 10:3 as the name of one of the descendants Japheth, son of Noah. From about the ninth century CE onwards Ashkenaz became identified with Germany in Jewish tradition. Later on, the name was applied to the Jews who lived in Germany and in the North-East of France. When, in the sixteenth century, German Jews moved eastward and settled in Poland and Lithuania the term Ashkenazim (plur of 'Ashkenazi') was applied to the Jews of these lands also. The majority of Ashkenazi Jews spoke Yiddish, which was basically a German dialect with many additions from Hebrew and from the Slavic languages. Ashkenazi Jews differ from Sephardi Jews (see box below) in the formulation of some liturgical texts, and in some customs and traditions. So, for example, some meat products which are accepted as kosher by Ashkenazi Jews may be forbidden in Sephardi communities. But the differences between the two branches of Judaism are not of major importance. From about 1800 many Ashkenazi Jews migrated to America and elsewhere. The vast majority of Hitler's Jewish victims were Ashkenazim. At present about 80% of the world's Jews belong to the Ashkenazi branch of Judaism.

Sephardi Jews

The place-name Sepharad, which occurs in Obad 1:20, was identified in Jewish tradition with Spain. Consequently Jews of the Iberian Peninsula and their descendants became known as Sephardim (plur of 'Sephardi'). The conquest of Spain by the Arabs in 711 marked the beginning of the 'Golden Age' of Spanish Jewry which produced many remarkable scholars. When the Jews were expelled from Spain in 1492 many of them settled in North Africa and in Turkey. Many Portuguese Jews emigrated to Amsterdam in the seventeenth century. The Sephardim spoke Ladino, a language that was basically Spanish with some loanwords from Turkish and Hebrew. The Sephardim differ from the Ashkenazim (see box above) in some details of the synagogue service and in some customs and traditions. At present about 20% of all Jews are Sephardim.

CHAPTER THREE

Sacred Texts of Judaism

THE HEBREW SCRIPTURES

It is often said that Judaism is a religion of the Book. However, if we are to accept this statement as true, we must understand 'the Book' to mean not just one book, but a vast body of literature that has been produced by many learned Jews over many centuries, and that has been diligently studied by countless Jews in every generation. This rich and varied literature has moulded the identity of the Jewish community, given expression to their deepest religious thoughts, defined the norms that govern their lives, and created the culture that is Judaism.

The kernel of this extensive literature, and the root from which it all grew, is the book, or collection of books, which Christians traditionally called the Old Testament. Nowadays many people prefer to use the term 'the Hebrew Scriptures' or 'the Hebrew Bible', since the term 'Old Testament' might seem pejorative, implying that the Hebrew Scriptures, are antiquated and outmoded.

The Jews distinguish three different sections in their Bible:
* The Law (*Torah* in Hebrew), the first five books of the Bible which were traditionally attributed to Moses.
* The Prophets (*Neviim* in Hebrew), which include the books from Joshua to 2 Kings inclusive.
* The Writings (*Ketuvim* in Hebrew) include Psalms, Proverbs, Job, Song of Songs, Ruth, Lamentations, Ecclesiastes, Esther, Daniel, Ezra, Nehemiah and 1-2 Chronicles.

By taking the initial letters of the words *Torah, Neviim* and *Ketuvim,* and by adding vowels, Jewish tradition constructed the word *Tanak* or *Tanakh,* and Jews frequently use this word to refer to the Bible.

The first division of the Bible, which Jews always refer to as the Torah, held a much more prominent place in Judaism, and had greater authority for Jews, than the other two sections. Jews believed that the Torah was directly revealed to Moses on Mount Sinai. This belief is based on texts like Exod 19:1 - 24:18 which describes the giving of the Ten Commandments to Moses, and Deut 4:44 which refers to 'the law (Torah) that Moses set before the Israelites'. See also Deut 33:4.

A number of books which form part of the Roman Catholic Old Testament are not found in the Hebrew Scriptures. Examples of such books are the Wisdom of Solomon, Ecclesiasticus, which is also known as Sirach, and 1-2 Maccabees.

Oral Torah

Besides the written word of the Bible the Jews also cherish the 'Oral Torah'. The Oral Torah clarifies and complements the written Torah that is to be found in the Bible. For example, the written Torah stipulates that Jews must keep the Sabbath holy (see Exod 20:8), but is the Oral Torah which specifies how one must observe the Sabbath, what work, for example, is allowed or forbidden on that day. Exod 12:1-14 describes how the Israelites celebrated the first Passover in Egypt, but it is the Oral Torah that established the ritual to be observed by later generations of Jews in their annual celebration of Passover.

Jews believe that the Oral Torah, like the written Torah, was revealed to Moses on Mount Sinai. But much of it, they say, was forgotten, and only later rediscovered by the Jewish scholars known as rabbis. When new situations required new legislation or new regulations the learned rabbis made the appropriate rulings. In doing so they claimed that they were drawing from the treasury of traditions that had been orally revealed to Moses on Mount Sinai. Rabbinic rulings of this kind are referred to in Mark's gospel as 'the tradition of the elders', 'the tradition of men', 'your tradition that you have handed on' (see Mk 7:3, 8, 13). What the rabbis wished to assert when they claimed that the laws they formulated had been revealed to Moses was that these

The Torah Scroll

Torah Scroll is the name given to the scroll that is used in the synagogue for the reading of the Torah (the Pentateuch) during certain
liturgical services. Such a scroll must be written by a specially trained
scribe who must follow very strict rules when writing the text. He
must use only specially prepared parchment from the hide of a ritually 'clean' or 'kosher' animal, and he must write with a quill from a
kosher bird, usually a goose or turkey, in black, durable ink. He must
employ a special script that is characterised by crown-like flourishes
at the top of certain letters. The same script is used in the writing of a
mezuzah and the *tefillin*. The scribe must copy his model text without
the slightest change. If a mistake is found in a scroll it must be cor-
rected before it can be used again for the Torah reading. A correction
is made by erasing the mistake with a knife or pumice stone, and by
replacing it with the correct reading. The strips of parchment on
which the text is written are stitched together so that they form a long
roll, the ends of which are wound around wooden rollers. By rolling
these in different directions one can move forwards or backwards in
the text. Handles of wood and flat wooden rollers are placed at the
top and bottom of the rollers to facilitate the rolling and the carrying
of the scroll. When the scroll is not being used the rollers are brought
side by side, tied together with a sash, and covered with an embroidered mantle. A decorated silver 'breastplate' or shield is suspended
from the handles over the front of the mantle. The 'breastplate' recalls
the breastplate worn by the High Priest (see Exod 28:15-30). Hanging
from the handles there is also a *yad*, 'a hand'. This is literally a hand,
usually in silver, with a pointing finger, and it is used to help readers
to follow the text exactly and to avoid mistakes. The use of the hand
ensures that a reader never touches the scroll with his or her finger,
something that is strictly forbidden at any time. The handles, mentioned above, are usually surmounted by two silver decorations, or
more usually, by a crown. If a scroll falls the congregation fasts from
dawn to dusk for forty days. This does not mean that the whole congregation fast for forty days. Individuals take it in turn to represent
the community over a period of forty days, excluding Sabbaths.
Everything about the Torah Scroll, the material on which it is written,
the way it is written, its ornamentation and its untouchable character,
are all calculated to stress its holiness and to create in the people a
sense of reverence for it.

laws, the Oral Torah, faithfully interpreted the Written Law, and that the Law of Moses and the laws of the rabbis formed one Law that obliged all Jews.

Jews can understand the word 'Torah' in three different ways:

- Torah = the first five books of the Bible.
- Torah = the whole Bible.
- Torah = the totality of God's revelation, that is, the Oral Torah and the Written Torah.

From the Babylonian Talmud

To understand the following text one must keep in mind that Shammai was a teacher who usually followed the stricter interpretation of the Jewish law, while Hillel was a master who usually took the more lenient view. As one can gather from the story, Hillel and Shammai were contemporaries; they lived at the end of the first century BCE and into the beginning of the first century CE.

> Our Rabbis taught: A certain heathen once came before Shammai and asked him, 'How many Toroth [plural of Torah] have you?' 'Two', he replied: 'the Written Torah and the Oral Torah.' 'I believe you with respect to the Written, but not with respect to the Oral Torah; make me a proselyte on condition that you teach me the Written Torah [only].' [But] he [Shammai] scolded and repulsed him in anger. When he went before Hillel, he accepted him as a proselyte. On the first day, he [Hillel] taught him, Alef, beth, gimmel, daleth [the first four letters of the Hebrew alphabet]; the following day he reversed [them] to him. 'But yesterday you did not teach them to me thus', he protested. 'Must you then not rely upon me [as to what the letters are]? Then rely upon me with respect to the Oral [Torah] too.'

THE MISHNAH

By New Testament times a large body of oral law had developed within Judaism, and from about that time it began to be put to writing. About 200 CE a learned rabbi called Judah the Prince collected and arranged the laws that were in circulation, in writing or orally, in his day, and published them in a book called the Mishnah. This work was to become the fundamental legal document of Judaism, and all later Jewish legal texts were based on it. The word 'Mishnah' comes from the Hebrew verb *shanah*, which has the basic meaning of 'repeat'. But because learning in Judaism at that time was by rote, that is, by repeated recitation, the word mishnah, came to mean 'learning' and 'teaching'. So the Mishnah is that book which contains the body of legal teaching that became authoritative in Judaism.

The Mishnah is divided into six parts called 'Orders' which formulate legal opinions on almost all aspects of Jewish life. The name of each Order suggests the main topic that is dealt with in that particular Order. The six Orders are as follows:

- *Seeds* begins with a chapter on prayer, and then deals with agricultural and related matters.
- *Holydays* (or Festivals) establishes the rules governing the observance of the Sabbath and the celebration of the Festivals, e.g. Passover, New Year, the Day of Atonement.
- *Women*, which deals with matters related to betrothal, marriage and divorce, the rights of a divorced woman or a widow, etc.
- *Damages* treats of different topics relating to civil and criminal law. The tractate Sanhedrin, which forms part of this order, deals, as the name indicates, with the constitution and working of the Sanhedrin, the supreme legislative Jewish body within Judaism. The tractate Pirke Avot is a collection of practical ethical maxims.
- *Holy Things* deals with the various kinds of sacrifices that were brought to the Temple, and with the rules governing the sacrificial system.
- *Purities*. This Order deals with ritual impurity, the ways it is

incurred and removed. Persons, vessels, utensils, garments etc, can become ritually impure. A corpse, a leper (see Lev 13-14, esp 13:45-46; Mt 8:1-4), an unclean animal, etc, can be a source of uncleanness. A special tractate deals with menstruation. Another tractate treats of the *mikveh*, the ritual bath in which men and women can purify themselves when ritually unclean.

Although the Mishnah is a code of rules that regulate Jewish life, it differs somewhat from a modern law code. Very often different opinions on a particular issue are given. Usually the less likely opinion (or opinions) is presented first, and this is followed by the authoritative view. The Mishnah often quotes the contradictory opinions of different rabbis and places them side by side, without deciding which opinion is to be accepted and followed. In other words, the Mishnah leaves many questions open, and it was the task of later scholars to debate the different opinions expressed in that authoritative work, and to decide how a Jew should act in a given set of circumstances. It is to be noted that the Mishnah contains many rulings that could not be put into practice at the time that document was edited. For example, the rules concerning Temple sacrifices were inapplicable at a time when the Temple no longer existed. For us who think of Rabbinic Judaism as a Torah-based system it may come as a surprise to learn that the Mishnah rarely uses biblical quotations to support an opinion or decision.

THE TOSEFTA

'Tosefta' is an Aramaic word meaning 'addition', 'supplement'. (Aramaic was the language spoken by Jesus.) The Jewish book known as the Tosefta is in reality an addition or supplement to the Mishnah. It was produced about the year 300, so about 100 years after the Mishnah. It is a collection of legal rulings and discussions arranged in the same six 'Orders' as the Mishnah. Although it contains much material that is very similar to parts of the Mishnah, it also deals with many topics that are not dis-

cussed in that work. The identity of the editor, or editors, is unknown. The Tosefta is four times as long as the Mishnah. It is
not, however, considered as authoritative as the Mishnah, and
whenever the former contradicts the latter the ruling of the
Mishnah is taken as normative. Unlike the Mishnah, the Tosefta
often quotes biblical texts to support its rules and its views.

THE TALMUD

After the publication of the Mishnah successive generations of
Jewish scholars studied it, analysed it and commented on it.
Study of this fundamental document took place not only in
Palestine, but also in Babylonia where there was a large Jewish
population. The text of the Mishnah, together with the comments and interpretations of many rabbis that were added to it,
became known as the Talmud. Put briefly, Mishnah plus commentary = Talmud. The commentary, as distinct from the
Mishnah, is known as the *Gemara*, an Aramaic word which
means 'completion'. It is worth noting also that unlike the
Mishnah which is in Hebrew, the *Gemara* is mostly in Aramaic.
The *Gemara* frequently quotes the biblical text or texts that form
a basis for a rule or proposition in the Mishnah.

Two versions of the Talmud developed, one in each of the
two centres just mentioned. The Palestinian Talmud, also known
as the Jerusalem Talmud, was completed around the year 400
CE, while the Babylonian Talmud did not reach its final stage of
development until the late sixth or early seventh century. The
Babylonian version, which is about three times as long as its
Jerusalem counterpart, was destined to receive wider dissemin-
ation and to become more authoritative in Jewish communities.
The Talmud is primarily a legal document that is largely composed of accounts of legal discussions in which casuistry and
hair-splitting feature prominently. But it also contains many
passages that give place to lively folktales, stories about individuals, maxims, medical advice etc.

Jews do not claim that the Mishnah, the Tosefta and the
Talmud are inspired by God. They regard these writings as the

product of the sharp intellects of rabbis who, over the centuries, tried to discover how God wanted the people he had called to be holy to live. The Mishnah and the Talmud, and to a lesser extent the Tosefta, continue to be diligently studied by religious Jews to this day. Because of the dedication of traditional Jewish scholars to these legal works, it has been said that Judaism was shaped less by theology ('learning about God') than by jurisprudence ('learning about the law'). But it was not only learned Jews who were committed to the laws of the ancestors. Ordinary Jews too treasured the Torah, delighted in putting it prescriptions into practice, and allowed it to fashion their way of life and their piety. By the early Middle Ages 'Judaism' was the Judaism of the Mishnah and the Talmud, the system that had been developed by the rabbis, and that continued to be interpreted by them and applied to every new situation in which Jews found themselves.

MEDIEVAL LAW CODES

The Talmud, which became the authoritative text to which Jewish leaders appealed when they sought a solution to legal or religious questions, is an extremely long document. In Hebrew it contains about 2.5 million words, on 5,894 folios or large pages. In a modern English version it runs to eighteen volumes of smallish print. It is not without reason that writers since the eighteenth century refer to 'the sea of Talmud'. Furthermore, the material is not ordered according to subject, with the result that the Talmud's teaching on a given topic must be found in different places in this vast body of literature. Another problem with the Talmud is that it leaves many issues unresolved. It often contents itself with presenting the views of different rabbis so that it offers no clear solution to some problems.

These drawbacks in the Talmud led later scholars to summarise its contents, to arrange its teaching according to topic, and to decide on practical resolutions to issues that remained unclear in the Talmud text. In other words, these scholars set about codifying Jewish law and making it more easily accessible to Jewish scholars, and through them to the ordinary people. The first efforts at codification began in the ninth century, but it was the code of Moses Maimonides (1135-1204), a work known as *Mishneh Torah* ('The Torah Recapitulated'), that became a standard text of Jewish law. The *Mishneh Torah* is in fact a statement of Jewish law in the clearest possible language. Other legal compendia were written during the following centuries. Among the most important of these was the *Shulchan Arukh* ('The Set Table'), which was published in Venice in 1565 by Joseph Karo. As the title suggests, the work was intended to prepare 'a well set table' where the contents of the law are clearly and attractively laid out for those who enter the banquet hall of Torah. This volume was destined to become an authoritative work on Jewish observance, and it is the code that has been most influential in determining the way modern Jews live out their Judaism. An abbreviated version of this popular volume was published in an English translation by H. E. Goldin under the title *The Jew and His Duties. The Essence of the Kitzur Shulchan Arukh* (New York: Hebrew Publishing Company, 1953).

A Story

The following text provides us with one of the best known little stories in rabbinic literature. On Shammai and Hillel who feature in the story, see above, page 51.

> On another occasion it happened that a certain heathen came before Shammai and said to him, 'Make me a proselyte, on condition that you teach me the whole Torah while I stand on one foot.' Thereupon he [Shammai] repulsed him with the builder's cubit which was in his hand [the cubit was a measure used to mark off the amount of work done by a builder]. When he went before Hillel, he said to him, 'What is hateful to you, do not to your neighbour (cf Mt 7:12): that is the whole Torah, while the rest is the commentary thereof; go and learn it.'

Shammai's rather rough treatment of the enquiring heathen was prompted by a suspicion that the questioner was merely mocking Judaism. As a scholar, Shammai knew that it takes many years to master the intricacies of the law, and that it was ridiculous to speak of learning it while standing on one foot. Hillel's reply does not water down the difficulties either. His principle that one must treat one's neighbour with love may sum up the whole Torah. But that does not excuse one from learning 'the rest' of the law which is a necessary 'commentary' on the basic commandment to love one's neighbour as oneself. The full implications of this commandment are spelled out in 'the rest' of the Torah.

MIDRASH

Besides the Mishnah, the Tosefta and the Talmud, which are primarily legal documents, Jewish scholars also produced commentaries on the Bible. The word for commentary in Hebrew is *midrash*, which is derived from a verb *darash*, a word that means 'search', 'examine'. The rabbis 'examined' the scriptures, that is, they studied them carefully, interpreted them, and produced commentaries on them that were intended to answer contemporary religious and ethical questions, and nourish the faith and devotion of the Jewish community. Many of these commentaries, or midrashim (plur of *midrash*) would have originated as actual homilies. Very often these midrashim included parables and fictional narratives that communicated religious and ethical teaching in an interesting and often entertaining way.

One commentary, or midrash, could be mainly legalistic – or halakic (see the box below: Halakah), if we wish to use the technical Hebrew term – while another could be primarily homiletic or haggadic (see the box below: Haggadah). Thus, for example, the commentary on Exod 12:1 - 23:19, a section of the Bible which contains much legal material, is mainly legalistic. This particular midrash, known as the *Mekilta de Rabbi Ishmael*, dates from before 300 CE. Similarly, a commentary on Leviticus, which is known as *Sifra*, is also legalistic. The core of this particular midrash may date back to the third century CE, although the text which now exists is the result of certain modifications and additions to this core text. On the other hand, the commentary on Genesis, known as *Genesis Rabbah*, which was written in the fifth century CE, is homiletic, or haggadic in character. It consists mainly of edifying interpretations, sometimes only loosely connected with the biblical text of Genesis. Midrashim, or commentaries on biblical books, continued to be written until the 11th or 12th centuries.

The following example illustrates how the compilers of the midrash applied Lev 26:9-12 to actual life situations in which the Jews found themselves. When Jerusalem and its Temple had been destroyed, and the Jews were exiled from their holy city, they felt that they had been abandoned by their God. But they were consoled and encouraged by the scriptural text which assured them that God would never cease to dwell among them:

> ... the heathens vex Israel by saying to them, 'Your God has hidden his face from you and removed his Shekinah [his Presence] from your midst; he will return to you no more.' They weep and sigh; but when they enter their Synagogues and Houses of Study, read in the Torah and find written therein, 'And I will look with favour upon you, and make you fruitful, and multiply you ... and I will place my dwelling in your midst ... And I will walk among you' (Lev 26:9-12), they are comforted.

Halakah

Halakah, literally 'walking', is the name given to the body of legal prescriptions that regulate the personal, social, and religious behaviour of Jews. Halakah extends to matters of civil and religious law, since Jews – whenever they had control of their own destiny – saw all law as religious. According to traditional Jewish teaching all the legal and ethical teachings of Judaism were communicated to Moses on Mount Sinai. Although the nucleus of the legal system that governs Jewish conduct is to be found in the scriptures, laws and regulations have continued to develop down through the centuries. Even today rabbinic authorities reinterpret the old halakah and formulate principles that enable people to respond to new problems and to changing circumstances.

Haggadah

Haggadah, or *Aggadah*: The word 'haggadah' has the basic meaning of 'narrative'. As a technical term it refers to a certain body of Jewish literature that comments on and amplifies the biblical text in a very imaginative fashion. The aim of this literature is to encourage ethical conduct, to edify, to offer comfort in times of trial, and to assure people that life lived according to the Torah will have its reward. In pursuit of these goals the creators of the haggadah used legendary accounts about the heroes of Israel's past (e.g. Moses, the patriarchs, kings, prophets), parables, dramatic dialogues, maxims, prayers etc. Their starting point was the scripture, but they used the biblical text very freely, adding fanciful developments to it, changing words to suit their purpose, and ignoring the limits of time and space so that anachronisms abound. Thus, for example, Abraham is said to have observed all the commandments, even though these were only revealed to Moses at a much later time. It is said that Jacob introduced the evening prayer although the custom of regular daily prayer was unknown until about the second century BCE. Although most haggadic material is to be found in the midrash, the Talmud also contains many haggadic elements. Stories from the haggadah are regularly used by contemporary Jewish preachers.

'The Haggadah' is also the name given to the book that contains the ritual for the Passover Seder.

THE TARGUMS

Aramaic was the primary international language of the whole of the Middle East from about 600 BCE. By the time of Jesus it was the major spoken language of Palestine. Many of Jesus' contemporaries would have had little or no knowledge of Hebrew, so that if they were to understand the Bible it had to be translated into their vernacular, that is, into Aramaic. Such an Aramaic translation was called a Targum. We know that Targums existed in Qumran, because Targums of the Book of Job and fragments of a Targum of Leviticus have been found there.

Much more important are the Targums that developed in the synagogue worship. The rabbis stipulated that during the course of the reading of the scriptures in the synagogal worship, the text would be read first in Hebrew, and then translated into

Aramaic. When the Torah text, that is a passage from the Pentateuch, was being read, the translator gave his rendering of each verse as it was read. In the case of a reading from the Prophets, he gave his translation after each three verses. This difference in the method of translation reflected the fact that the reading from the Pentateuch was much more important than the prophetic text. Since the Targum was clearly distinct from the sacred text of the Torah (Pentateuch), the translator felt free to interpret the passage that was being read in the light of contemporary theology, and to apply it to the life situations in which the Jews found themselves. In the actual synagogue service, the translator could not use a written translation, and he could not look at the Hebrew text being read. The reason for these stipulations was that the translation, which was regarded as part of the Oral Torah, had to be seen to be clearly distinct from the Written Torah, and it could not be written down. Gradually, however, the translations were put to writing, so that several versions of the Targum to the Pentateuch, as well as a Targum of the rest of the Bible, have come down to us.

As an example of the kind of free 'translation-interpretation' we sometimes find in the Targums, we may take the following Targum of Gen 40:9-12. According to vv 5-8, Joseph's fellow-prisoners told him that they had a dream which no one could interpret. Joseph asked them to tell him their dreams, and volunteered to interpret them. At this point (v 9) we take up the Targum text, placing the original biblical words in ordinary Roman script, and putting the translator's additions in italics:

9. And the chief cup-bearer told his dream to Joseph and said to him: 'In my dream behold there was a vine before me. 10. And on the vine there were three branches. And it bloomed; it sent out blossoms, the clusters ripened and *became* grapes. 11. And Pharaoh's cup was in my hand and I took the grapes and pressed them into Pharaoh's cup, and I placed the cup in the palm of Pharaoh's *hand*.' 12. And Joseph said to him: 'This is its interpretation: The three branches are the three *fathers of the world: namely, Abraham, Isaac, and Jacob, the sons of*

whose sons are to be enslaved in the slavery of the land of Egypt and
are to be delivered by the hands of three faithful leaders: Moses
Aaron and Miriam, who are to be likened to the cluster of grapes.
And as regards what you said: 'I took the grapes and pressed them
into Pharaoh's cup and I placed the cup in the hands of Pharaoh',
this is the cup of retribution which Pharaoh is to drink in the end.

Joseph's far-fetched 'interpretation' of the dream is based on the
imaginative claim that the three branches mentioned in the
dream (v 10) represent the three Patriarchs, Abraham, Isaac and
Jacob. The clusters of grapes that grew on the vine (v 10) are seen
as pointing to the three leaders of the Exodus period, Moses,
Aaron and Miriam. Pharaoh's cup (v 11) is taken to symbolise
the 'cup of God's wrath' (see Is 51:17) which was to be poured
out on Pharaoh, the wicked oppressor. However fantastic this
'interpretation' may be, it was intended to communicate a message of hope and encouragement to Jews who may have been
the victims of injustice and persecution, and who had to put
their trust in God who would deliver them from their sufferings
and who would punish their enemies.

THE PRAYERBOOK

We include the Prayerbook among the Sacred Texts of Judaism,
firstly, because it is, in its own way, a compendium of Jewish
theology and spirituality and, secondly, because, after the Bible,
it is the book that is most familiar to ordinary Jews. It is popularly
known by its Hebrew name, the *Siddur*, 'the order of prayers'.
The earliest prayerbooks included prayers for public and private worship for Sabbaths and Festivals. Nowadays, the *Siddur*
contains mainly the prayers for the Sabbath and weekday services, while the order of service for the Festivals is found in a
volume, or in volumes for individual Feasts, known as the
Mahzor.

The *Siddur*, as it exists today, is the result of a long history of
liturgical development. Generation after generation has added
its own prayers, hymns and readings to what for many centuries

was a fluid collection of prayers. In the early Christian centuries the rabbis forbade the writing down of prayers, and the leader of the congregation was expected to know the prayers by heart. Although some collections of prayers were in existence by the eighth century CE, the first known version of the Prayerbook was published in Babylon in about the year 860. In the following centuries other prayerbooks were produced in different localities. While all of these contain the same basic material, each of them contains special texts that reflect local rites and customs. A certain standardisation took place in the English speaking world when Simeon Singer published the *Authorised Daily Prayerbook* in 1890. There have been several editions of this volume, and it is still used in some Orthodox synagogues in England and Ireland. Nevertheless, since the early 1800s, different strands of Judaism, Orthodox and progressive, have produced a great variety of prayerbooks, and the process of adapting and modifying the ancient *Siddur* shows no sign of abating.

WOMEN AND THE TORAH

In the opening chapter of the Bible we are told that 'God created humankind in his image, in the image of God he created them; male and female he created them' (Gen 1:27). It is clear that for the author of this statement man and woman were of equal dignity in the presence of God at the moment of creation. But a little further on in Genesis we read that the woman was told that her husband would rule over her (3:16). The writer of this verse came from a society where male dominance was accepted as normal, and where women were accorded an inferior status. This was, in fact, the kind of society that is known to us from the Hebrew scriptures. It is true that some biblical women held positions of leadership in ancient Israel. We read, for example, of Miriam, who on one occasion was called a prophetess (Exod 15:20-21), and who on another occasion joined Aaron in speaking out against Moses because of the Cushite woman whom he had married (Num 12:1). Deborah was a prophetess, a judge, and one who directed Barak who led Israel's army to victory

(Judg 4-5). Jael is celebrated as the courageous woman who killed the leader of the enemy forces by driving a tent-peg through his temple (Judg 4:17-22). Huldah was a prophetess (2 Kings 22:14), and the Book of Esther tells how a woman, Esther, through her courage and diplomacy managed to rescue a Jewish community that was threatened with extinction. Nevertheless, the women of ancient Israel were rarely in the limelight, their place being in the home and in the kitchen.

The scholars who formulated the classical texts of Rabbinic Judaism were part of a world that was decidedly patriarchal, a world in which women lived very much in the shadow of their husbands. Furthermore, these classical texts are the product of a literate male elite, who fully accepted the values of the man's world in which they lived. In these texts, women are seen through the eyes of men, and female voices are rarely heard directly. This does not mean that women are presented in an unfavourable or negative light in rabbinic literature. The rabbis, for example, would approve of the image of the ideal wife – efficient housekeeper, industrious, kind, generous, enterprising – as portrayed in Prov 31:10-31. But even in this positive portrayal, the praiseworthy woman is still seen as a subordinate, and the reins of authority are firmly in the hands of the husband. The woman's status stems from her important role in the home and in family life, and from the contribution she makes to her husband's well-being.

Nevertheless, the rabbis did not regard a man's wife as a mere housekeeper or servant who was expected to perform certain duties within the home. They saw her as one who had her own dignity, one who had a right to respect and honour. They said: 'Concerning a man who loves his wife as himself, who honours her more than himself ... Scripture says: "You will know that your tent is at peace"' (Job 5:24). 'One must always observe the honour due to his life, because blessings rest on a man's home on account of his wife.' A husband should keep in mind that a woman is very sensitive, and he must be careful not to hurt her. The Talmud expresses this idea as follows: 'One should always be heedful of wronging his wife, for since her tears are frequent she is quickly hurt.' Sentiments like those must be kept in mind when we read other statements that seem to reduce the wife to a mere servant of her husband. Maimonides (d. 1204), for example, says: 'The sages commanded the woman to honour her husband to excess, and she should fear him; all her actions should conform to his wishes, and she should regard him as a minister or a king.'

That women's personal rights were limited may be gathered from the fact that they are sometimes mentioned with slaves and minors in the Mishnah and in the Talmud. So, for example, the Mishnah states that 'Women, slaves and minors are exempt from the recital of the *Shema* and the *Tefillin*.' Women, slaves and minors are not obliged to pay the half-shekel Temple tax. The Talmud states explicitly that where the observance of precepts is concerned, women and slaves are on the same footing: 'Every precept which is obligatory on a woman, is obligatory on a slave; every precept which is not obligatory on a woman is not obligatory on a slave.'

The Mishnah lays down the general principle that 'All positive ordinances that are bound up with a stated time are incumbent upon men but women are exempted.' Women, for example, are not obliged to attend the communal synagogue worship or to recite the *Shema* because these obligations must be fulfiled at a fixed time. Exemption from these observances is based on the assumption that her duties in the home make it difficult for a woman to observe them.

The Rabbis of old regarded women as a possible occasion for unchaste thoughts on the part of men. The Talmud states that a woman's uncovered leg, her hair, her voice were enticements to sin. It declares that a man should not walk behind a woman on the road. The Talmud gives no reason for this proscription, but one can conclude that female sexual seductiveness was not far from the mind of the man who made it. The Rabbis of the Talmud were so sensitive to the seductiveness of women that they forbade a man to count money from his hand into the hand of a woman so as to have the opportunity of gazing at her face. Even in the synagogue women could be a source of distraction for men, and it is for this reason that during liturgical services female worshippers took their place either in the balcony or behind the *mehitzah*, the partition or screen that separated them from men. Since it was forbidden for men to listen to women's singing, it is only in recent times that progressive synagogues have allowed mixed choirs.

A saying in the Talmud that inevitably surprises one who hears it for the first time runs as follows: 'A man is bound to say the following three blessings daily: '[Blessed are you ...] who has not made me a heathen ... who has not made me a woman ... who has not made me a brutish man.' This triple blessing has been incorporated into the Prayer Book, and it holds its place there, in one form or another, even today. It must be admitted that the reference to a woman in this blessing has a decidedly negative and pejorative ring about it. However, from the context in which the saying occurs in the Talmud, it is clear that a man who thanks God for not having made him a woman, is giving thanks for the fact that, as a man, he is given the privilege of observing certain precepts from which a woman is exempt. In fact, the Jerusalem Talmud says explicitly: 'It is said, Blessed be He who has not made me a woman, because the commandments have not been entrusted to a woman.' Nevertheless, when a modern reader comes upon the prayer in question in the daily Morning Prayer, he or she is taken aback by its tone of male superiority. It is true that traditional Prayer Books add an alternative version that may be recited by women while men thank God for their own male status. So the woman thanks God 'who has created me according to his will'. In our gender-conscious world this sounds like the prayer of one who is resigned to a situation that is undesirable but inescapable. It is not surprising then that modern versions of the Prayer Book change the traditional formula that sounds like a remnant from a patriarchal society. The Conservative Movement, for example, has replaced the old negative wording with a purely positive one: '... who has made me an Israelite ... a free person ... and in His image'.

In traditional Judaism women were exempt from the precept of studying Torah. The rabbis based this exemption on the fact that Deut 11:19 (Hebrew text) obliges a father to teach his sons (NRSV: children) Torah. Since only sons are mentioned in this verse, the rabbis concluded that there is no need to teach daughters. As a result, few Jewish women received an education that would enable them to study the rabbinic literature that so engaged their menfolk. Religious education for girls focused mainly on preparing them for the responsibility of running a Jewish home according to the traditional rules. They were, for example, obliged to become familiar with the laws of kosher and with the customs that governed the celebration of the religious festivals in the home. Since most women could not read Hebrew they depended on vernacular texts for the nourishment of their spiritual lives. A book known as *Tseenah U-Reenah* became a favourite for many women in Eastern Europe. This Yiddish work, which was written in the 1590s, was a paraphrase of the weekly texts that were read in the synagogue, together with selections from popular commentaries from the Middle Ages.

One of the consequences of the traditional separation of the sexes was that women were deprived of rights that should have been theirs. They were never, for example, called to read the Torah before a congregation in the synagogue, never served as a prayer leader in the liturgical services, and never counted as members of a *minyan*. In the nineteenth century the promoters of the Reform Movement, who believed in the equality of the sexes, questioned the justice of this situation, and in order to prepare women for fuller participation in Jewish life they began to give the same religious education to boys and girls.

In the early twentieth century Jewish women from the wealthier classes were becoming involved in philanthropic activities, as well as in the domestic management of synagogues and in teaching in synagogue religious schools. But it was only in the 1960s, and under the influence of the feminist movement in the non-Jewish world, that women manifested their unwillingness to accept their peripheral role in the Jewish religious community. Not satisfied with the traditional image of the woman as mother and home-maker, and as the person who was responsible for the moral values of the family, they demanded equality in the synagogue. Their efforts were not in vain, and their struggle for women's rights brought about dramatic changes within Judaism. In 1972 the Reform Movement ordained the first woman rabbi. The Reconstructionists followed suit and ordained their first woman rabbi 1974. The first Conservative female rabbi was ordained in 1985. At present more than half of the students entering the rabbinical seminaries of the Reform, Conservative and Reconstructionist movements in the United States are women. The Orthodox community does not allow the ordination of women. But many Orthodox women are pursuing advanced studies in the highest institutes of Jewish religious education, and a number of female Orthodox scholars continue to bring a female point of view to bear on matters of Jewish theology, law and ritual.

While the ordination of women may be the most dramatic result of the feminist movement within Judaism, that movement has resulted in many other changes in Jewish life. In the area of liturgy, for example, we may mention that Reform communities abolished the women's gallery by the end of the 1800s, and men and women worshipped on the same floor. Nowadays all the Jewish movements, except Orthodoxy, allow women to be counted in the *minyan*. One practical result of this is that women can now take their place among the mourners who recite the mourner's Kaddish at daily communal prayers during the year after the death of a close relative. Formerly it was only men who performed this traditional duty. The wording of some liturgical texts had been altered in the light of feminist sensitivities. Whereas older English translations of the Jewish Prayer Book were formulated in masculine terms, more recent versions, especially those in use in non-Orthodox communities, use inclusive language. The language used to refer to God includes masculine and feminine terms and metaphors, and prayers and readings are couched in gender-inclusive terms.

Some new rituals that celebrate aspects of women's lives have been introduced. The celebration of the birth of a baby girl now parallels the rite of circumcision for a boy, and *bat mitzvah* forms a counterpart to *bar mitzvah*. Some women's groups are now introducing new rituals and liturgies to mark *Rosh Hodesh*, the new moon, or the beginning of the lunar month. Traditionally this day was observed as a kind of woman's holiday on which only the necessary household chores were performed. In general it can be said that the feminist movement has brought about many changes in Jewish life, in synagogue leadership, in theological thinking and in ritual.

CHAPTER FOUR

Important Jewish Festivals: An Overview

It has been said that their religious calendar was the catechism of the Jews. The annual cycle of feasts commemorated the historical events that formed Israel as the people of God, and the liturgical texts read in the liturgical celebrations of the great Feasts gave expression to the people's religious beliefs and convictions. The yearly celebration of the feasts introduced children to the religious heritage and to the traditions of the Jewish people, and at the same time nourished the faith of adults and strengthened their sense of Jewish identity. Judah Halevi (d. 1141), a famous Jewish poet and philosopher, stated that the festivals were the main factor that helped the Jews to survive as a people among the Gentiles.

In the Jewish calendar one can distinguish between feasts that are mentioned in the Pentateuch and those that were added later. Feasts mentioned in the Pentateuch are:

- *Passover and Unleavened Bread*, which are treated in Judaism as one festival.
- *Weeks and Tabernacles*. These feasts, together with Passover/ Unleavened Bread, are known as the three 'Pilgrim Festivals'.
- *New Year and the Day of Atonement*. These two form a pair, in the sense that New Year begins a ten-day period of repentance which finishes at the end of the Day of Atonement. These two feasts are often referred to in English as the High Holidays.

The more important of the later festivals are:

- *Purim*, which celebrates events that are recorded in the Book of Esther.

- *Hanukkah*, which commemorates the rededication of the Temple by the Maccabees (see 1 Macc 4:36-59).
- *Simchat Torah, 'Rejoicing in the Law'*. According to Lev 23:36 and Num 29:35, the eighth day of the Feast of Tabernacles is to be a day of 'solemn assembly', and no work is to be done on it. But no special reason is given for the celebration. Sometime after 600 CE the day became known as *Simchat Torah*, a joyful celebration in honour of the Torah. The practice of reading the whole Pentateuch in the synagogue in the course of a year was well established by then, and the annual reading was completed on *Simchat Torah*. This is the case also at present, and on this day, on *Simchat Torah*, the final chapters of Deuteronomy are read in the synagogue, and these are followed by the reading of the first chapter of Genesis. Thus one cycle of synagogal reading ends, and a new one begins. It is considered a special honour to be called to read either the portion from Deuteronomy or the portion from Genesis on this occasion. To mark the Jews' delight at having finished the cycle of Torah readings, and to express their thanks to God for the gift of the Torah, all the Torah scrolls which the synagogue possesses are carried around the synagogue to the accompaniment of singing and dancing and merrymaking. In Israel *Simchat Torah* is celebrated on the eighth day of Tabernacles. In the Diaspora it is celebrated on the following day.
- *The Ninth of Ab*, which is a commemoration of the destruction of Jerusalem, is an important day of mourning and penance.

Pilgrim Festivals

The 'Pilgrim Festivals', mentioned above, get their name from such passages as Exod 23:14-17 and Deut 16:16 which specify that on the three great feasts of Passover/Unleavened Bread, Weeks and Tabernacles, all males must 'appear before the Lord', that is to say, they must present themselves at his sanctuary. Until the end of the seventh century BCE this obligation could be fulfilled at local sanctuaries, but after that time all had to go to

Jerusalem. The Pilgrim Festivals were the three most important feasts of the year, and they were closely connected with the agricultural year. Passover/ Unleavened Bread took place at the time of the barley harvest, Weeks at the time of the wheat harvest, and Tabernacles at the fruit harvest. But in Israel these agricultural feasts were 'historicised', that is, they were interpreted as memorials of events in the history of Israel (see Passover, Feast of Unleavened Bread, Feast of Weeks, Tabernacles).

The High Holidays

New Year's Day, known in Hebrew as *Rosh Hashanah*, and the Day of Atonement, or, to give it its Hebrew name, *Yom Kippur*, became known in rabbinic tradition as the 'Days of Awe', and in modern times they are often referred to in English as the High Holidays. They are undoubtedly the most solemn festivals of the Jewish religious calendar. The days from New Year (1st Tishri [Sept-Oct]) to the Day of Atonement (10th Tishri) are known as the 'Ten Days of Repentance'. According to rabbinic teaching these ten days provide the sinner with the best opportunity for repentance.

Rosh Hashanah and *Yom Kippur* are much more synagogue-centred than the other major festivals. The liturgies are much longer, and even Jews whose links with the synagogue and its liturgy are tenuous attend the services on these days.

Minor Festivals

The feast of *Purim* is celebrated on the 14th of Adar (Feb-March) as a commemoration of the victory of Esther, a beautiful Jewish woman, over Haman, the wicked prime minister of the King of Persia who had decided to exterminate the Jews. The name *Purim* is derived from the word *pur*, meaning 'lots', and it refers to the fact that Haman cast lots in order to fix a date on which he would destroy the Jewish people (see Esther 3:7-14). Scholars today agree that the story of Esther, which is recorded in the biblical Book of Esther, is fictional. The feast of *Purim* has always been, and still is, more a folk festival than a religious celebration.

This is in the spirit of Esther 9:19 which states that the feast is to be 'a day for gladness and feasting, a holiday on which they send gifts of food to one another'. During the reading of the Book of Esther on the feast it is customary for the congregation to boo, stamp their feet and make plenty noise with a rattle each of the fifty-four times the name 'Haman' is mentioned in the reading. During the afternoon a festive meal takes place. Special pastries known as *Hamentaschen*, 'Haman's pockets', are eaten. These are triangular in shape, and they are filled with poppy-seeds and dried fruits. It is customary at Purim to send gifts to friends and to the poor, and it is also the practice to give money, 'Purim money', to children. Down through the centuries, when the Jews were threatened by hostile rulers, they were consoled and encouraged by the story of Esther's victory over the powerful Haman.

If Purim is associated with the legendary exploits of Esther, Hanukkah, as noted above, commemorates a historical event, the victory of the Jews over the Greeks and the following rededication of the Temple which took place in 164 BCE (1 Macc 4:36-59). It is an eight-day festival, beginning on the 25th Kislev (December). Since the Books of the Maccabees were not included in the canon of the Hebrew Scriptures, Hanukkah is the only important Jewish holiday that has, according to Jewish reckoning, no basis in the scriptures. It is therefore not surprising that the rabbis do not seem to have considered Hanukkah an important feast. The Mishnah, besides mentioning the feast in passing on several occasions, refers to Hanukkah lights. In the Talmud we find the legend which tells that when the Jews came to rededicate the Temple, they found only one jar of pure oil, enough for one day's lighting. However, when they lit the lamp, a miracle happened, and the lamp continued to burn for eight days. It was this legend that gave rise to the custom of lighting Hanukkah lights on a menorah for eight days. Candles are lit each night after sunset. On the first night one candle is lit, and a candle is added on each of the following nights. This candle-lighting ritual is by far the most important feature of the Hanukkah celebration.

By the Middle Ages Hanukkah had become a popular festival, and in modern times, especially in Israel, it has become a symbol of the courage of the Jews in the face of hostile powers. Since Hanukkah occurs in December the feast has taken on some of the festive spirit of Christmas, especially in America where it is a kind of Jewish counterpart to the Christian feast. It is customary to give gifts, especially to children, during the feast. A custom that has been traditionally associated with Hanukkah is the spinning of the *dreidel*. This is a four-sided spinning top which has a Hebrew letter inscribed on each of its sides. Each letter stands for a Hebrew word, and the four words read together give the sentence 'a great miracle happened there'. In modern Israel this formula is slightly altered to give the reading 'a great miracle happened here'. The reference is, of course, to the miracle of the oil mentioned above.

Day of Mourning

According to the Mishnah 'the Temple was destroyed the first and the second time' on the ninth of Ab (July-August). Every reader of the Mishnah would immediately know that the text referred to the destructions of 586 BCE and 70 CE. According to tradition, the expulsions of the Jews from England (1290) and from Spain (1492) also took place on the ninth of Ab. To this day the tragic loss of the Temple is commemorated on the 9th Ab by a fast lasting from sunset to sunset. Other penitential practices are also observed on this day, and other signs of grief are displayed. It is forbidden to wear leather shoes (as on the Day of Atonement); one should not wash or anoint oneself; spouses should refrain from sexual intercourse; study of Torah is forbidden since this would be a source of joy. In the synagogue only minimal lighting, enough to enable one to read the prescribed texts, is allowed. Texts read during the service are the Book of Lamentations, which laments the destruction of Jerusalem, passages from Job, and lamentations from the Middle Ages which were composed on the occasion of some persecution to which the Jews were subjected. However, the day of mourning is not

one of total despair, as we gather from the following prayer for
the day which looked forward to the rebuilding of Jerusalem:

> Comfort, O Lord our God, the mourners of Zion, and the
> mourners of Jerusalem, and the city that is in mourning, laid
> waste, despised and desolate. ... Legions have devoured her,
> worshippers of strange gods have possessed her ...
> Therefore let Zion weep bitterly. ... For you, O Lord, did con-
> sume her with fire; and with fire you will in future restore
> her. ... Blessed are you, O Lord, who comforts Zion and re-
> builds Jerusalem.

'You Shall Rejoice'

The major feastdays were occasions of great rejoicing and celebration. The Bible states explicitly that people must rejoice at the
Feast of Weeks (Deut 16:11, 14), at the Feast of Tabernacles (Lev
23:40) and at the Feast of Unleavened Bread (Ezra 6:22). Neh 8:17
shows that the Feast of Tabernacles was celebrated with rejoicing after the return from the Exile in 538 BCE, as were Passover /
Unleavened Bread (see Ezra 6:22) and 'the first day of the seventh month', that is, the New Year (see Neh 8:2, 9-12).

The rabbis declared that 'Rejoicing on a Festival is a religious
duty', and they explained that one can fulfil this duty by devot-
ing half of the day to eating and drinking, and the other half to
the study of the sacred texts. The general principle was that one
must 'honour the Festivals and delight in them just as one honours and delights in the Sabbath'. So, one should cut one's hair
'in order not to inaugurate the Festival with an untidy appear-
ance'. One should bathe in warm water, comb one's hair and
pare one's nails. One should bake hallah for the Festival, just as
one does for the Sabbath. One should give presents to one's family and dependants. On feastdays one should also provide food
for the needy. The Bible (Neh 8:9-12) attests to the custom of
showing practical concern for the poor on the occasion of the festivals.

CHAPTER FIVE

Jewish Feasts in Brief

FEAST	DATE	BIBLICAL BASIS
New Year (Rosh Hashanah)	1st of Tishri (Sept-Oct)	Lev 23:24-25
Day of Atonement (Yom Kippur)	10th of Tishri (Sept-Oct)	Lev 23:26-32
Feast of Tabernacles (Sukkoth)	15th of Tishri (Sept-Oct)	Lev 23:33-43
'Rejoicing in the Torah' (Simchat Torah)	23rd Tishri (Sept-Oct) (= 8th day of Tabernacles)	See Num 29:35
Hanukkah	25th Kislev (December)	1 Macc 4:36-59
Purim	14th of Adar (Feb-Mar)	Book of Esther
Passover (Pesach) Unleavened Bread (Matzoth)	14th Nisan (March-April) – 21st Nisan	Exod 12:1-27
Feast of Weeks (Pentecost)	6th Sivan (May-June). Seven weeks after Passover	Lev 23:15-16
Ninth of Ab	9th Ab (July-August)	—

NEW YEAR: ROSH HASHANAH

There is no explicit mention of a New Year feast in the Hebrew
Bible. Indeed, the whole dating system during the early Old
Testament period is unclear. According to one reckoning the
year began in spring, when the Feast of Passover was celebrated.
The month in which this festival took place is called 'the first
month' (Exod 12:2; Lev 23:5). In another source we are told that
the Feast of Tabernacles was 'the festival of harvest ... the festival of ingathering at the end of the year' (Exod 23:16). The end of
one year was, of course, followed by a new year. In later Judaism
Tishri (September-October) – the seventh month of the year that
began with Nisan – was universally regarded as the first month.

The Bible describes the first day of Tishri as a feast day to be
'commemorated with trumpet blasts' (Lev 23:23-25; Num 29:1-
6). This is the day that is regarded by Jews as the beginning of
the New Year. In the Mishnah it is called Rosh Hashanah, the
name by which it is known today by English-speaking Jews.
According to the Bible the festival lasts only one day. Since Jews
who lived in the Diaspora could not be easily informed about
the time when the new moon (and, therefore, the new month)
occurred, they observed the feast on two days in order to ensure
that it would be celebrated on the right day. But even in Israel,
since the Middle Ages, Rosh Hashanah is a two day celebration.

New Year Observances

As noted above, Lev 23:24 prescribes that the first of Tishri, the
New Year feast, be 'commemorated with trumpet blasts'. In obedience to this precept the shofar is solemnly blown on the feast.
The blowing of the shofar is, in fact, the most recognisable feature of the day. The liturgy refers to the New Year as 'this day of
memorial, a day of blowing the horn'. Although the shofar is
blown on many different occasions during the year it is sounded
with special solemnity and according to strict rules at the New
Year. Maimonides (d. 1204), in a frequently-quoted passage, explains the blowing of the shofar at the New Year as follows:

...the sounding of the shofar on Rosh Hashanah ... has an

intimation, as if to say: 'Arise from your slumber, you who are asleep; wake up from your deep sleep, you who are fast asleep; search your deeds and repent; remember your Creator. Those of you who forget the truth because of passing vanities, indulging throughout the year in the useless things that cannot profit you nor save you, look into your souls, amend your ways and deeds. Let everyone give up his evil way and his bad purpose.'

Although some Jewish authorities claimed that the world was created in Nisan, the accepted view was that it was created in Tishri, and at the New Year God is celebrated as Creator. He is proclaimed in the liturgy of the day as 'supreme King of Kings ... who stretched forth the heavens and laid the foundations of the earth'. The feast itself is referred to in a prayer as 'This day, on which was the beginning of your work, is a memorial of the first day.'

New Year's Day is also considered as a day of judgement, the day when, as the Mishnah states, 'all that come into the world pass before him [God] like legions of soldiers [to be judged]'. During the sounding of the shofar a liturgical passage which is addressed to God says 'this day you cause all the creatures of the universe to stand in judgement ...'. According to the Talmud, three books are open on New Year's day: one for those who are entirely wicked whose names will be immediately inscribed into the book of death; one for the wholly righteous whose names will be written into the book of life; and one for those who are in between. Judgement on this latter group will be suspended until the Day of Atonement, which occurs ten days later. The liturgy for the festival states that at New Year 'sentence is pronounced upon countries, which of them is destined to the sword and which to peace ... and each separate creature is visited thereon, and recorded for life or for death'.

But this day of judgement is not a mournful day. On the contrary, people dress in white, and the decorations in the synagogue (e.g. the covers of the Torah scroll, the hanging before the Torah shrine) are white, symbolising the conviction that God will purify his people. The white clothing and a festive meal express the joy of the festival.

In the afternoon of the first day of the feast some Jews go to a place where there is flowing water, and emptying their pockets or shaking their robes, symbolically 'cast' their sins into the water. The custom (called *tashlik*) is based on Micah 7:19: 'You will cast all our sins into the depths of the sea.' Another form of this ritual is to cast bread crumbs, which represent one's sins, into the water. The practice of *tashlik* seems to have originated in Germany in the fourteenth century. It is a reminder that New Year begins a ten-day period of repentance which ends on the Day of Atonement.

The Torah readings for the day include the birth of Isaac (Gen 21) and the sacrifice of Isaac, which the Jews prefer to call the Binding of Isaac (Gen 22). The story of the birth after Sarah's long barrenness (Gen 11:30; 16:1), and the rescue of Isaac from sacrificial death, add a hopeful note to the celebration. The story of the Binding of Isaac is particularly relevant on this feast, because the rabbis taught that the merits of Abraham, who willingly offered his son, and the merits of Isaac, who freely offered himself as a victim, would tip the scales in favour of Israel at the moment when they would be judged by God.

Three Special Themes

Among the special features of the New Year is a series of three prayers that reflect three important themes of Jewish theology. The first of these celebrates God's universal sovereignty over the world and over humans; the second recalls how God remembers the deeds of nations and individuals, rewarding the good and punishing the wicked. This God, who showed his kindness and fidelity to his chosen people in the past, will continue to remember them with favour in the future; the third mentions events in Israel's history that are linked with the blowing of the shofar, and it looks forward to the final redemption of the people. Towards the end of this third blessing we read the following lines:

Our God and God of our fathers, sound the great Shofar for our freedom. ... bring our scattered ones among the nations near unto you, and gather our dispersed from the ends of the earth. Lead us with exultation unto Zion your city, and unto Jerusalem the place of your sanctuary with everlasting joy.

At the evening meal at the beginning of New Year it is customary to dip a piece of hallah (the special kind of white bread that is eaten on the Sabbath) in honey and to say, 'May it be your will, O Lord our God to renew unto us a happy and pleasant year.' A piece of apple is also dipped into honey and a similar prayer said. At New Year people greet each other with the words 'May you be inscribed (in the book of life) for a good year.'

A Prayer

As mentioned earlier, one of the themes that is celebrated on the Feast of the New Year is that of God's kingship. The following prayer from the Evening Prayer with which the feast begins, expresses a longing for the manifestation of God's universal kingship:

We therefore hope in you, O Lord, that we may speedily behold the glory of your might, when you will remove the abominations from the earth, and the idols will be utterly cut off, when the world will be perfected under the kingdom of the Almighty, and all peoples will call upon your name, when you will turn unto yourself all the wicked of the earth. Let all the inhabitants of the earth perceive and know that unto you every knee must bend, every tongue must swear. Before you, O Lord our God, let them bow and fall prostrate; and unto your glorious name let them give honour; let them accept the yoke of your kingdom, and reign over them speedily, and for ever and ever. For yours is the kingdom, and to all eternity you will reign in glory.

The Shofar

The Shofar is a ritual musical instrument which is made from an animal's horn. The Hebrew word *shofar* occurs about seventy times in the Hebrew Bible, and it is translated as 'trumpet' (see e.g. NJB and NRSV Exod 19:16) or as 'ram's horn' (see e.g. NJB Ps 47:5), or simply as 'horn' (see e.g. NJB and NRSV Ps 98:6). Modern English-speaking Jews usually leave the Hebrew word untranslated.

According to the Bible the shofar was blown on a great variety of occasions. It was sounded, for example, when the Lord spoke to Moses on Mount Sinai (see Exod 19:16, 19); when Joshua circled the walls of Jericho (Josh 6:1-21); it roused soldiers in time of war (see e.g. Judg 3:27); it was blown by watchmen (cf e.g. Jer 6:17), and it was used to proclaim the Jubilee Year (see Lev 25:9-10) and to call the people to repentance (see Joel 2:1).

In contemporary Judaism the shofar is sounded on the first day of the New Year, a day which is referred to in the Bible as 'a day for you to blow the trumpets' (Num 29:1). It is blown at the end of the Day of Atonement, on fast days, and in Orthodox communities it is sounded to announce the beginning and end of the Sabbath.

To fulfil the commandment to sound the shofar one may use the horn of a sheep, a goat, a mountain goat, an antelope, a gazelle. The horn of a cow, a bull or an ox is not allowed because of the shameful incident of the Golden Calf (Exod 32:1-6). The rabbis favour the use of a ram's horn because it can serve as a reminder of the ram that replaced Isaac when he was about to be sacrificed by his father (Gen 22).

THE DAY OF ATONEMENT: YOM KIPPUR

The Day of Atonement, which occurs on the tenth of Tishri (Sept-Oct), that is ten days after the New Year, is, without doubt, the holiest day of the Jewish year, a day of utmost solemnity. It is usually referred to, even in modern languages, by its Hebrew name, Yom Kippur. There is no reference to this feast in any biblical text that pre-dates the Exile (586 BCE), but the basic elements of the feast may have been in existence before that time. The days between Rosh Hashanah and Yom Kippur are known as 'the ten days of repentance'.

Chapter 16 of the Book of Leviticus lays down the rituals that are to be performed on Yom Kippur. The day is 'a sabbath of solemn rest' (v 31), a day on which all forms of work are forbidden. Only on the Day of Atonement is the High Priest – referred to in this chapter as Aaron – allowed to enter the Holy of Holies (v 2). Dressed in linen clothes (v 4), and not in his usual elaborate vestments, he offers sacrifices to make expiation for his own sins and those of the priestly house (vv 6, 11, 17), as well as for the sins of all the people (vv 15-19). He sends the scapegoat, to whom the sins of the whole nation were symbolically transferred, into the wilderness (vv 20-22). On this day all the people must 'deny themselves', and they must do no work (v 29). This is the day on which atonement is made for all their sins (v 30). This is an annual ritual which takes place on the tenth of the seventh month (v 29), which is Tishri. According to Num 29:8-11, the day was marked by the offering of special sacrifices. The Mishnah tractate Yoma, 'the Day [of Atonement]', gives detailed instructions for the carrying out of the various rituals that were to be performed in the Temple on that day.

Yom Kippur in the Synagogue

Before the Fall of Jerusalem (70 CE) the Day of Atonement was primarily a Temple ceremony. While the Temple stood, the observance of Yom Kippur was, as we have just seen, a matter of carrying out certain rituals and offering prescribed sacrifices. But when the Temple was destroyed, and when its sacrificial and ritual systems had come to an end, a new importance was given to the role of the people, to their confession of sin, to their repentance and to their desire for forgiveness. Since that time Yom Kippur has become the day when Jews everywhere repent of their sins, humble themselves before God, and ask pardon for their sins. On this day even those Jews who are usually negligent about religious observance participate in the synagogue services, and many Jews spend most of the day in the synagogue. The mood of this day of repentance and confession is expressed in a prayer that occurs during the evening liturgy with which the day's observance begins:

> Our God, and God of our fathers, may our prayer come before you, and do not withdraw from our supplications; for we are not so shameless or so hardened as to declare in your presence, O Eternal our God, and God of our fathers, that we are righteous, and have not sinned. We have trespassed, we have dealt treacherously, ... we have acted perversely, we have transgressed. ... What shall we say in your presence, O you who dwells on high.

Kol Nidre

The celebration of the day begins with a festive meal on the evening of the ninth of Tishri. After the meal the people go to the synagogue where, just before sundown and while it is still daylight, the prayers begin with a solemn proclamation known as *Kol Nidre*, 'All Vows'. The gist of this prayer may be gathered from the following few lines:

> All vows, obligations, oaths ... or any other expression by which we shall have vowed, sworn, devoted, or bound ourselves to, from this Day of Atonement, until the next Day of Atonement ... we repent beforehand of them all; they shall be deemed absolved, forgiven, annulled, void, and made of no effect ...

The origin of this rather curious formula is unknown. According to one school of thought it may have originated in the ninth or tenth century. Taken at face value, it seems to declare, in anticipation, that all vows and oaths that a Jew may make during the year ahead are invalid and without binding effect. For this reason many Jews over the centuries have objected to this ritual prayer, and some non-Jews have claimed that it makes all Jewish oaths and all Jewish evidence worthless. But the rabbis explain that *Kol Nidre* refers only to vows that have been made to God, and that it does not apply to oaths made in a secular law court. At another level the Mishnah makes it clear that offences against one's neighbour are forgiven on Yom Kippur only if one is reconciled with the neighbour in question: 'For transgressions that are between a man and his fellow the Day of Atonement effects atonement only if he has appeased his fellow'. The *Kol Nidre*, which is in Aramaic, and not in Hebrew, the usual language of the traditional liturgy, is one of the most characteristic elements of the ceremonies of the Day of Atonement. It is sung to a moving traditional air, and it has been popular in Judaism for centuries.

Later in the ceremony there is an elaborate formula of confession of sins. A similar formula is also recited at each of the four services on the Day of Atonement. This solemn confession begins as follows:

You know [O Lord] the mysteries of the world, and the hidden secrets of all the living. You search all the inward parts, and you examine minds and hearts; so that there is nothing concealed from you, neither is there anything hidden from your sight. O may it be acceptable in your presence, O Lord our God and God of our fathers, to pardon us all our sins, to forgive us all our iniquities, and to remit all our transgressions.

'You Shall Deny Yourselves'

From the beginning of the opening evening service, which we have just described, until the end of the Day of Atonement, that is, for a period of twenty-five hours, 'eating, drinking, bathing for pleasure, anointing, putting on shoes, and marital intercourse are forbidden'. The basis for the imposition of these forms of self-denial is the biblical command 'you shall deny yourselves' (Lev 23:27; Num 29:7). Instead of 'putting on shoes (of leather)' people sometimes wear such things as cloth slippers or gym shoes. The prescription regarding footwear is often ignored in non-Orthodox congregations. The twenty-five hour fast is the most characteristic observance of the Day of Atonement. Those who are sick and women who are pregnant are not obliged to observe the fast. When Luke refers to 'the Fast' in Acts 27:9, he has the fast of the Day of Atonement in mind.

In the course of the long service on the morning of the day of the feast a confession of sins, like that of the previous evening is repeated, traditional hymns are sung, and Lev 16, Num 29:7-11 (a list of the sacrifices that were offered in the Temple on the Day of Atonement), and Is 57:14-58:14 (which includes statements about the nature of true fasting) are read.

Avodah

The second service of the day, the so-called 'Additional Service', contains a lengthy account of the ritual that was carried out in the Temple before its destruction. This account – known as the *Avodah*, which may be translated as 'The Order of the Temple Service' – was originally a description of the Temple ritual for the Day of Atonement as it is known to us from Lev 16 and the Mishnah. This description was greatly expanded by many poets over the centuries. Different versions, some as late as the year 1000, exist. The reading of the *Avodah* is regarded by many as the most moving element of the Atonement service, since it reminds the people of the solemn services and sacrifices of the ancient Jerusalem Temple. It has been said that the *Avodah* prayer recalls a Temple ceremony that involved the holiest person among the Jewish people (the High Priest), a ceremony that took place on the holiest day in the Jewish year (Yom Kippur) and in the holiest place in the Jewish world (the Holy of Holies). Recalling the glories of the ancient Temple on Yom Kippur is a very emotional experience for Jews, and the plaintive melodies to which the liturgical texts are set add to its attractiveness.

The Book of Jonah

The main feature of the afternoon service, the third service of the day, is the reading of the Book of Jonah, which describes how the people of Nineveh were forgiven by God when they responded to the preaching of Jonah and publicly repented of their sins. The phrase which makes the book particularly appropriate for the Day of Atonement occurs in 3:10: 'When God saw ... how they (the Ninevites) turned from their evil ways, God changed his mind about the calamities that he had said he would bring upon them (the people of Nineveh)'. If God forgave the repentant Ninevites, he would surely forgive his repentant people. Micah 7:18-20, a passage which praises God as one who pardons iniquity and delights in mercy, is also read.

Neilah

The fourth and final service of the day, which is known as *Neilah*, 'Closing', begins about an hour before sundown. According to some scholars the term *Neilah* originally referred to the ancient ceremony of closing the Temple doors in the evening of the Day of Atonement. Others think that the reference is simply to the closing of the gates of heaven which were open until the very end of the day for those who wished to repent. Like the other services of the day, *Neilah* contains confessions of sin and urgent appeals for forgiveness, as may be illustrated by the following lines which play on the images of closing the gates of heaven and, as it were, being given a last chance to win God's forgiveness:

> Oh, have mercy upon us ... for you, O God, are a merciful and gracious King. Oh, open the gate for us at this time of closing the gate; for the sun declines. The day declines, the sun goes down and begins to vanish; Oh, let us enter your gates. O Omnipotent ... forgive, pardon, have compassion, have mercy upon us. ... Accept our prayers in mercy and favour. Our Father and our King, open the gates of heaven to our prayer.

This leads up to a dramatic moment when the leader begins the

Shema and solemnly proclaims 'Hear, O Israel: the Lord our God, the Lord is One' (Deut 6:4). All present proclaim three times 'Blessed be his glorious, sovereign Name forever and ever', the response which, according to the Mishnah, the people made when the High Priest pronounced the divine name in the Temple on the Day of Atonement. Then the leader and all present repeat seven times 'The Lord he is God' (see e.g. Deut 4:35, 39), beginning with a whisper and gradually raising their voices. After this impressive ritual, a final prayer, the Kaddish, is recited, and a long blast of the shofar announces the end of the solemn day of penitence, and indeed the end of the whole ten days of repentance. Immediately the usual evening prayer is said and a new day begins.

Some Customs and Beliefs
Some traditional Jews go to the *mikveh* on the eve of Yom Kippur to symbolise the purification that this solemn day will bring. As at New Year, it was customary to wear a long white robe on the Day of Atonement, and only white hangings and drapes were used in the synagogue on that day. The purpose of this practice was to symbolise the purity which the people wished to acquire (cf Is 1:18) by means of the day's observances.

A custom which is known from about 900 CE, and which was popular among Orthodox Jews in many places until recent times, was that of taking a cock (for a male) or a hen (for a female) on the eve of the feast and swinging it three times over one's head while reciting the formula: 'This is my substitute, my vicarious offering, my atonement; this cock (or hen) shall meet death but I shall find a long and pleasant life.' The fowl, which, it was believed, would then bear any misfortune that might result from one's sins, was then killed and given to the poor.

It was believed that Satan, who could bring accusations against Israel before God on all other days of the year, could not do so on Yom Kippur.

On this day, judgement is passed on those who are neither completely righteous nor completely wicked, and whose fate was left undecided at the New Year (see New Year). If they repented during the ten days since New Year they are now inscribed in the book of the righteous; if not, they are inscribed with the wicked.

The Jew's conviction that his or her sins were forgiven on the Day of Atonement is expressed in these words which occur towards the end of the concluding service of the day:

Blessed are you, O Lord, our king who pardons and forgives our iniquities and the iniquities of your people the house of Israel, and who makes our trespasses to pass away year by year: King over all the earth, who sanctifies the Day of Atonement.

However, the fruits of the day were available only to those who truly repented of their sins. The Mishnah states explicitly that 'If a man said, "I will sin and the Day of Atonement will effect atonement," then the Day of Atonement effects no atonement'.

THE FEAST OF TABERNACLES

The Feast of Tabernacles, or Booths, was the third of the 'Pilgrim Festivals'. Since the Hebrew for 'Tabernacles' is *sukkoth*, Jews usually refer to this feast as 'Sukkoth'. It was a seven-day celebration, beginning on the fifteenth day of the seventh month (Lev 23:33-34), the month of Tishri, which corresponds to Sept-Oct in our calendar. In Exod 23:16 it is called 'the festival of ingathering at the end of the year', a suitable title for a feast that celebrated the end of the wheat harvest and the harvesting of the produce of the vineyard (Deut 16:13). In other texts (e.g. Lev 23:34) it is referred to as the 'feast of booths (or tabernacles)', a title which points to the particular feature that was to become the central custom of the festival, namely, the practice of living in booths, or tabernacles, during the seven days of the festival (Lev 23:42). Originally a 'booth' (Hebrew *sukkah*) was a simple shelter made from branches and covered with leaves. It was erected in a vineyard and served as a shelter for a watchman who protected ripening grapes (see Is 1:8; Job 27:18). In biblical times, Tabernacles was considered the most important celebration of the year. It could be referred to simply as 'the festival' (1 Kings 12:32).

Since the Feast of Tabernacles marked the end of the harvest season it was a particularly joyful celebration (Lev 23:40; Deut 16:14-15). The branches referred to in Lev 23:40 seem to have been carried and waved in a happy procession of harvest revellers. The feast is referred to in the Jewish liturgy as 'the season of our rejoicing'. It was originally purely agricultural, but it was later given a historical significance and regarded as a commemoration of the forty years during which the Israelites wandered in the wilderness and dwelt in tents (Lev 23:42-43).

Water Libation

The Mishnah describes a ritual of 'water-drawing' that took place in the Jerusalem Temple at the end of the first day of the Feast of Tabernacles, and in the evenings of the remaining days, except for the Sabbath. Water from the Pool of Siloam (see Jn 9:11) was carried in procession into the Temple to the accompaniment of the blowing of the shofar and the playing of various musical instruments. At the altar a priest took the water and poured it on the altar. The rite was carried out so that rain might be plenty in the coming year. It is against the background of this ritual that Jn 7:37-39 is to be understood.

The ritual of the 'water-drawing' was carried out in a particularly cheerful mood. Rabbinic texts describe how pious and learned men, with burning torches in their hands, used to dance and sing songs of praise, while countless Levites played a variety of musical instruments and two priests sounded trumpet blasts. The rabbis said that anyone who had never experienced this joyful occasion had never seen joy in his/her life. When the Temple was destroyed this ritual ceased to be practised. In recent times, however, efforts are being made to revive it.

Post-Biblical Times

Two biblical commands, 'You shall live in booths' (Lev 23:42), and 'you shall take branches' (Lev 23:40), provided the basis for two important features of the celebration of Tabernacles in post-biblical times. In obedience to the command to 'live in booths' all males, excluding infants and slaves, are obliged to live in a booth during the seven days of the festival. The 'booth' is a temporary dwelling erected in the open, beside one's home. The Mishnah lays down detailed rules about its dimensions and the manner of its construction. Basically, however, the booth is a temporary structure with four walls, usually made of wood, or of canvas suspended on a frame, and covered with branches. The rabbis lay down that the booth should be decorated with tapestries and with various fruits, e.g. almonds, peaches, pomegranates, etc. During the seven days of the feast the booth must be regarded as one's home, and one must eat and sleep in it. In cold and rainy climates this law is not applied strictly.

Lev 23:40 commands the Israelites to take branches of different kinds, and to rejoice before the Lord. Two trees, the palm and the willow, are mentioned explicitly in this verse, and the rabbis took 'the fruit of goodly trees' to be the citron, and they understood 'the boughs of leafy trees' to be branches of myrtle. These four, the palm, the willow, the citron and the myrtle, are referred to in rabbinic literature as the 'Four Species'. The citron, which is a lemon-like fruit, is more commonly known among Jews by its Hebrew name *etrog*. Sprigs of myrtle, willow and palm were bound together to form what was known as the *lulav*. (Although the Hebrew word *lulav* is sometimes used to refer to the palm, it is more commonly taken to mean the ritual object that is formed by binding the palm, the willow and the myrtle together.) While the Temple stood, the *lulav* was carried in the right hand, and the citron in the left, as the people went in procession within the sacred precincts on each of the seven days of the feast. This ritual was regarded as fulfilling the prescription of Lev 23:40, the text mentioned above. When the Temple was destroyed the custom was continued in the synagogue. At a certain point in the synagogue service the people waved the *lulav* in each of the four directions, as well as upwards and downwards.

This ritual waving was a form of prayer for rain, a summons to the four winds to bring the rain that would ensure fertility in the coming year. The waving of the *lulav* in all four directions also symbolises God's universal sovereignty.

On each of the first six days of the feast, during the morning service, the worshippers, carrying the *lulav* and the citron, make one circuit round the sanctuary. While doing so they recite hymns known as the *Hoshanot*. This name comes from the fact that the hymns begin with the word *hoshana*, 'save us'. On the seventh day, again carrying the *lulav* and the citron, the worshippers make seven circuits of the synagogue while reciting the *Hoshanot*.

The first day and the last day of the feast are solemn festivals on which no work is allowed. On the days in between, the 'Intermediate Days', (see Unleavened Bread), only essential tasks may be performed. On the eighth day of Tabernacles, the feast of *Simchat Torah*, 'Rejoicing in the Torah', is celebrated in Israel. Elsewhere Orthodox and Conservative Jews celebrate *Simchat Torah* on the following day.

Customs

People often invite guests, especially friends or neighbours who may be living alone, to join the family in the booth during the feast. Besides these ordinary guests, seven spiritual 'guests' are invited to join the company for the whole seven days of the festival. The seven are Abraham, Isaac, Jacob, Moses, Aaron, Joseph and David. All seven were at some time exiles or wanderers, just as the Israelites were wanderers for forty years in the wilderness. The biblical texts that refer to the exile of the seven are Gen 12:1 (Abraham); 26:1 (Isaac); 28:1-2, 5 (Jacob); 37:36 (Joseph); Exod 2:15 (Moses); Aaron accompanied Moses during the forty year' wandering in the wilderness; David fled from Saul (1 Sam 19:10). Nowadays, some people also invite the matriarchs (Sarah, Rachel, Rebecca, Leah) and other heroines of Israel's history (Miriam, Esther etc). The people in the *sukkah* are encouraged to treat each of those 'guests' as if they were really present, and they should study the biblical texts that refer to them.

PASSOVER

The Passover, as we know it from the Bible and from Jewish tradition, has its roots in a springtime festival, which was celebrated by nomadic shepherds before the people of Israel ever came into existence. As the shepherds prepared to move their flocks from their winter grazing places to summer pastures they sacrificed a young animal to win divine protection for themselves and their flocks. The Israelites adopted this springtime feast and transformed it into a celebration of their own liberation from Egypt. The fullest biblical account of the Israelite celebration of the feast is to be found in Exod 12:1-14. This passage refers several times to the lamb that was offered, as well as to unleavened bread and bitter herbs (v 8), which form essential elements of the feast to this very day.

The month in which Passover is celebrated is called 'the beginning of months' (v 2). The phrase 'the beginning of months' means 'the most important month', and the month's importance comes from the fact that it was during this month that Israel's liberation from Egypt took place. It was then that Israel as a people was born. The Feast of Passover celebrates this great event, and it is to take place on 'the fourteenth day of this month' (v 6). To this day Jews celebrate Passover on the fourteenth of Nisan, a month which corresponds to the end of March and early April in our western calendar. This day is for all Jews 'a day of remembrance' (v 14), a day in which they relive the liberation that took place in Egypt long ago. Verses 11-12 (also vv 26-27) explain that the word 'Passover' (*Pesah* in Hebrew; the 'h' in *Pesah* is pronounced like 'ch' in Scottish 'loch') refers to the fact that the Lord 'passed over' the houses of the Israelites and struck the houses of the Egyptians with the tenth plague.

A Temple Celebration

The Passover sacrifice was originally celebrated by individual families, but we have no way of knowing whether the ritual took place in peoples' homes or in local shrines. However, we learn from the Book of Deuteronomy that by the seventh century BCE animal sacrifices, including the sacrifice of the Passover lamb, were permitted only in the Temple of Jerusalem. Deut 16:1-8 specifies that the Passover must be offered 'in the place that the Lord will choose as a dwelling for his name' (v 2), that is to say, in the Jerusalem Temple. Thus Passover ceased to be a domestic rite and became part of the ritual of the Temple. This explains why Jesus and his parents went to Jerusalem every year to offer the Passover sacrifice and to eat the Passover meal there (see Lk 2:41). Pilgrims like the Holy Family had to find a place in Jerusalem where they could eat the Passover meal when their Passover victim had been sacrificed in the Temple. Jesus and his disciples were faced with the same problem (see Mk 14:12-14). Pilgrims could buy animal victims from traders in the Temple area (see Jn 2:13-16). When the Temple was destroyed by the Romans in 70 CE, sacrifice could no longer be offered in Jerusalem, and people had no reason to make a Passover pilgrimage to the Holy City. Once again, therefore, Passover became a domestic ritual, and individual families celebrated the feast in their own homes.

The Passover Ritual

At one time the Feast of Passover was distinct from the Festival of Unleavened Bread (see e.g. Lev 23:5-6). At a later stage the two feasts were combined, so that in the New Testament the term Passover can sometimes refer to the combined Passover/Unleavened Bread Festival (see e.g. Lk 2:41; 22:1). On other occasions Passover refers specifically to the Passover meal (see Mt 26:18). In our present context we are dealing solely with celebration of the Passover on the evening of the fourteenth of Nisan.

We have no direct information about the ritual that surrounded the Passover meal at the time of Jesus, when, of course, the Temple sacrifices were still being offered. From the gospel accounts which imply that the Last Supper was a Passover meal (see e.g. Mt 26:17-30), we gather that eating the Passover lamb and Unleavened Bread, drinking wine and singing hymns or psalms formed part of that ritual. 'Bitter herbs', that is, vegetables or plants of some kind, probably dipped in some kind of sauce, would also have been part of the meal. This would be in accord with the biblical stipulation (see Exod 12:8). We can be sure that some form of blessing was recited over the Passover lamb, over the bread and over the wine, since blessings over food were common in Judaism of the time. It is most probable that some instruction about the Exodus and its meaning also took place during the course of the meal. The Bible itself requires that such instruction be given at the Passover celebration (see Exod 12:26-27; 13:8).

The Mishnah gives some instructions about the way in which the Passover is to be celebrated. It also includes some prayers and other formulae that may form part of the celebration. The ritual which contemporary Jews follow at Passover has its roots in the Mishnah text. But, of course, the text has been changed in many ways, and many additions have been made to it in the course of centuries.

Since the Temple no longer exists, and consequently, sacrifice is not possible, the Passover lamb has no place in the ritual. The Hebrew word for the ritual order which is followed in the Passover celebration is *Seder*, and this is the word by which the Passover meal with its prayers and rituals is now popularly known. However, there are no formulae which are everywhere obligatory, and local communities can introduce their own scripture texts, psalms, prayers, narratives and songs etc. A book containing the prayers, blessings, psalms, songs and legends that are read at the Seder is known as a Haggadah, a Hebrew word which actually means 'narrative'. The central theme of the Passover narrative is the liberation of the Israelites from the slavery in Egypt. For this reason, Passover is referred to in the liturgy as 'the season of our liberation'. But the Passover is not just a commemoration of an event that took place three thousand years ago. It is rather an experience in which every Jew who celebrates the Passover participates. This idea is expressed in a short passage, but a key passage, in the Passover Haggadah:

In every generation, one must look upon oneself as if one had come forth from Egypt, as it is said: 'You shall tell your children on that day saying, "It is because of what the Lord did for me when I came out of Egypt"' (Exod 13:8). For it is not alone our forefathers that the Holy One, blessed be He, redeemed. He redeemed us too, with them, as it is said: "He brought us out from there in order to bring us in to give us the land that he promised on oath to our ancestors"' (Deut 6:23).

The Passover celebration is a means of handing on Israel's faith experience to succeeding generations. For that reason children are given an important place in the ritual. So, for example, the youngest child at the table asks the so-called 'Four Questions', one of the best known features of the celebration. The four questions ask for an explanation of four important features of the ritual: unleavened bread, bitter herbs, dipping vegetables and reclining.

Passover Symbols

The immediate preparation for the celebration of Passover begins with the removal of everything leavened from one's house on the morning of the fourteenth of Nisan. After mid-morning, and for the following week, that is, until the end of the Feast of Unleavened Bread, it is forbidden to eat anything leavened. The Hebrew word for unleavened bread is *matzah* (plur *matzoth*), and this is the word Jews regularly use to refer to it. *Matzah* is a flat bread, like a cracker, whose only ingredients are flour and water, and that is made from dough that has not been allowed to ferment.

In the evening of the fourteenth, the Passover table is set as for an elaborate festive meal. The best available table cloth and table ware, candles and flowers set the scene for a joyful celebration. The most important Passover symbols are placed on a Seder plate at the centre of the table. These include:

Three pieces of Unleavened Bread (*matzah*). On every Sabbath two loaves are placed on the Table. The third piece of *matzah* that is added at the Passover meal points to the special importance of that feast. According to tradition the three pieces of *matzah* represent the three divisions of the Jewish people: Priests, Levites and Israelites. The *matzah*, eaten in the context of the Passover meal, is a reminder of the fact that the escaping Israelites had no time to allow their dough to ferment (see Exod 12:34). It is therefore aptly referred to in the Passover Haggadah as 'the bread of affliction' (see Deut 16:3). Every participant in the Passover meal is obliged to eat at least a minimum portion of *matzah*. This obligation is based on Exod 12:8 which states 'they shall eat it [the Passover sacrifice] roasted over the fire with unleavened bread and bitter herbs'.

Bitter herbs, usually represented by horseradish, are a reminder of the bitterness of the slavery in Egypt (see Exod 1:14). The practice of eating bitter herbs is also based on Exod 12:8 which we have just quoted with reference to the duty of eating unleavened bread at the Passover meal.

A vegetable, such as parsley or lettuce. It is dipped in salt water near the beginning of the meal. The vegetable is a symbol of spring and new life; the salt water is a reminder of the tears that were shed by the Israelites during their slavery in Egypt.

Fruit purée, called *charoset*, made, for example, from apples, walnuts, cinnamon and moistened with red wine, serves as a reminder of the mortar with which the Israelite slaves made bricks for their Egyptian masters.

A roasted shank bone is symbolic of the Passover lamb that was offered in the Temple. Since the Temple was destroyed in 70 CE it has been impossible to continue that sacrificial offering. The fact that the bone is roasted is a reminder that the Passover lamb was roasted (see Exod 12:8).

A hardboiled or roasted egg is a symbol of fertility and renewal. When roasted it is also a reminder of the special offering, besides the Passover lamb, that was brought to the Temple on the eve of Passover and eaten at the afternoon meal. Since eggs traditionally formed part of the meal of mourners on their return from the cemetery after a burial, the egg on the

Passover table is also seen as a symbol of mourning for the
Temple in Jerusalem.

Wine, a symbol of joy, is drunk four times during the Seder.

The Cup of Elijah, a specially decorated goblet or glass, is set
for the prophet Elijah who, according to popular belief, was
expected to return at Passover to announce the coming of the
Messiah.

Many Versions of the Haggadah

In our day many different types of Jews, from the ultra-conserv-
ative to the totally secular, celebrate the Passover. Orthodox
Jews, as well as many other Jews who are of a traditional mind-
set, retain the full text of the Haggadah as it has been handed
down for centuries, and they sing with gusto the folk-songs that
have become part of the Passover celebration. Not content with
the lengthy story of Israel's liberation from Egypt as it is narrated
in the Haggadah, they add their own explanations and comments. They may apply the Passover story to contemporary issues such as the liberation of today's oppressed, or the political
problems facing the State of Israel in our day. They take seriously
the words of the Haggadah which state that 'whoever expands
upon the story of the Exodus deserves praise'.

Jews of more liberal tendencies freely adapt the text of the
Haggadah and relate it to contemporary experience. While re-
taining the central themes of the Exodus story they may replace
some of the traditional readings with texts, reflections and
prayers which they find more relevant to the lives of Jews today.
They encourage individual participants to offer their own insights into the meaning of the Exodus experience in today's
world, and to reflect on the light it might cast on contemporary
political and social problems.

Then there are secular Jews for whom terms such as Exodus
and redemption have lost their religious connotation. They too
celebrate the Passover, and in doing so they see themselves as
part of the Jewish people whose ancestors were rescued from
the Egyptian slavery. They create their own Haggadah, as it

The Menorah in the Terenure synagogue. The Menorah as described in the Bible was a seven-branched lampstand that stood in the Temple in Jerusalem. After the destruction of Jerusalem in 70 CE, a custom developed of not making an exact replica of the Temple Menorah. This explains why the Menorah reproduced above has eight lights. One notices also that the lights are not candles or traditional oil lamps but electric bulbs. For more on the Menorah, see below p 122.

The interior of the Terenure synagogue, looking towards the back. In the foreground one sees the seating for men, and in the rear is the women's gallery (see below, pp 118-119). To the right stands the *bimah* (see below, p 117).

The Ark or Torah Shrine in the Terenure synagogue, Dublin. When not in use the Scrolls are stored in the Ark behind the crowned animal figures. The two Hebrew letters over these figures are the initials of two words that mean 'Crown of Torah'. This term refers to a crown-like ornament that is placed at the top of a Scroll when it is not being used. The twelve figures, six on each side of the central animal figures, represent the twelve tribes of Israel. The two tables of the Law are depicted over the Ark.

The Terenure Hebrew Congregation Synagogue, Rathfarnham Road, Dublin, was opened in 1953. In 1999 the members of the Adelaide Road synagogue amalgamated with the Terenure congregation. The Terenure synagogue is an Orthodox establishment, although not all members are strictly observant to the highest Orthodox standards.

The Ark or Torah Shrine. Part of what is now the Irish Jewish Museum in Walworth Street, South Circular Road, Dublin, was a synagogue from 1917 until the 1940s. The old synagogue is preserved within the museum. The Ark of the synagogue contains two Torah Scrolls, each wrapped in a richly decorated 'mantle'. The Hebrew inscription over the Ark reads, 'I keep the Lord always before me' (Ps 16:6).

Torah Scroll. The scroll above, which is said to have come from Lithuania in the late 1880s when many Jews from that country settled in Dublin, is preserved in the ark of the old synagogue. On Torah Scrolls in general, see above, p 50.

The Adelaide Road Synagogue in Dublin was built in 1892 in what has been called 'a vaguely Byzantine style'. The building was extended in the 1920s. Due to declining membership the congregation merged with the Terenure congregation in 1999, and the synagogue was sold for approximately £6,000,000. It is now part of a new office block complex.

פ נ

איש ישר כ' יצחק בר שמואל
נפטר ביום ב' י"ט לחדש תשרי
שנת תרמ"ג לפ"ק
ת נ צ ב ה

IN LOVING MEMORY
OF
JOHN ISAAC DAVIS
WHO DEPARTED THIS LIFE
ON THE
19TH DAY OF TISHRI 5643
AGED 79.
DEEPLY MOURNED BY HIS
SORROWING CHILDREN.

MAY HIS SOUL REST IN PEACE.

HARRISON   DUBLIN

The Jewish Cemetery in Ballybough, Dublin, served as the burial place for the Jews of Dublin from 1718 until 1900. The inscription on the tomb above, which commemorates a man who died in 1882 (5643 in the Jewish reckoning) uses formulae that are common on Jewish funerary monuments. The two Hebrew letters at the top stand for words that mean 'Here Lies'. The five letters at the end of the Hebrew inscription mean 'May his/her soul be bound in the bundle of life' (see 1 Sam 25:29).

were, as they focus on the social, political and humanitarian lessons that can be learned from the Exodus story.

For every Jew, whatever his or her religious belief, whatever his or her association with Jews and Judaism for the rest of the year, Passover is a high point in the annual calendar. According to the traditional Haggadah, one ended the Passover meal with a prayer that looked forward to future celebrations:

The Passover seder is ended,

According to custom, statute and law.

As we have been found worthy to celebrate it this year,

So may we be found worthy to celebrate it in future years.

O Pure One, dwelling in your habitation,

Take and lead the saplings of your stock –

Redeemed with joyous song – to Zion,

Next year in Jerusalem.

THE FEAST OF UNLEAVENED BREAD

The Feast of Unleavened Bread, *matzoth* (plur of *matzah*) in Hebrew, begins with the Passover meal at which unleavened bread is eaten, and continues for a period of seven days (Lev 23:5-6). It seems that the feast had its roots in a pre-Israelite agricultural festival, and that it celebrated the beginning of the grain harvest, that is to say, the barley harvest. It is mentioned as an independent seven-day feast in Exod 23:15, and again, in very similar terms, in 34:18. According to these texts it was celebrated in the month of Abib (March-April), a month which was later known in the Jewish calendar as Nisan. But no specific date in Abib is given for the feast, probably because the date depended on the time of the ripening of the harvest. The feast was, as we learn from Exod 23:14-15, one of the 'Pilgrim Festivals'.

Several texts mention the Feast of Unleavened Bread in association with Passover. Some of these, e.g. Lev 23:4-8 and Num 28:16-25, still treat the celebrations as distinct festivals. Others combine the two celebrations and treat them as one. Deut 16:1-8, for example, merges the two feasts, and treats Passover/Unleavened Bread as a pilgrim feast that must be celebrated in Jerusalem, which is referred to as 'the place that the Lord your God will choose' (vv 2.5-7).

It is not altogether clear how or when Passover – which was originally a family celebration (see Exod 12:3.21-23), and which involved only the offering of a sacrifice and the sharing of one solemn evening meal – was combined with the Feast of Unleavened Bread, which was one of the Pilgrim Feasts, and which lasted seven days. The fact that both feasts took place in the month of Nisan, and that the eating of unleavened bread was a feature of both celebrations, would have facilitated the merger. But whatever may be said of the history of the two feasts, the New Testament shows that by the beginning of the Christian era they were regarded by many as constituting one festival (see e.g. Lk 22:1).

Observing the Feast

In Jewish communities Passover and the Feast of Unleavened Bread are regarded as one celebration. According to biblical tradition both feasts commemorated Israel's liberation from Egypt. Exod 12:17 explicitly states that the Feast of Unleavened Bread is a memorial of the Exodus. The eating of unleavened bread during the festive period of Passover / Unleavened Bread is a reminder of the fact that in their hurry to leave Egypt the Israelites 'took their dough before it was leavened' (Exod 12:34).

The characteristic feature of the feast is the exclusion of anything leavened from people's diet during the seven days of the feast (Exod 12:15). The only bread that is allowed is unleavened bread (*matzah*), that is, bread that had been baked in such a way that it has not fermented. The positive duty of eating unleavened bread applies only to the Passover meal. This obligation is based on Num 9:11: 'they shall eat it [the Passover sacrifice] with unleavened bread and bitter herbs'. On the seven days of the feast one must abstain from eating leaven, but one is not obliged to eat unleavened bread. Unleavened bread may be eaten all during the year, but it has become customary not to eat it for the month preceding Passover so that its novelty might be appreci-

ated during the feast. Not only are Jews forbidden to eat anything leavened, but the mere possession of it is forbidden.
Consequently, traditional Jews who may trade in leavened
foodstuffs, sell them to a Gentile for the duration of the festival
on the understanding that the Jew will buy them back again
after the holiday. For the rabbis 'the yeast in the dough' was
seen as a symbol of the tendency to evil that is within human beings, a tendency that prevents people from doing the will of
God. The same idea is found in the New Testament reference to
'the leaven of malice and evil' (1 Cor 5:8). Within Judaism, the
abstention from leaven during the period of Passover/
Unleavened Bread became a symbol of the moral integrity to
which the Jew should strive.

The first day and the last day of the feast are holy days (Exod
12:16), and on these days all work is prohibited. On the
'Intermediate Days', the days between the first day and last day
of the feast, only essential work, e.g. preparing meals and caring
for the sick, was permitted. Regulations governing what may or
may not be done on these days are laid down in the Mishnah
tractate *Moed Qatan*, a term which means 'Lesser Feast'. Today,
most Jews work as usual on the 'Intermediate Days'. They do,
however, refrain from eating leavened bread on those days.

On the 'Intermediate Days' special readings are added at the
morning prayer in the synagogue. On the first of these days, for
example, Exod 13:1-16, which deals with the institution of the
Feast of Unleavened Bread, is read.

THE FEAST OF WEEKS

The Feast of Weeks is the second of the Pilgrim Festivals (see
Important Jewish Festivals). Its name, which occurs in Exod
34:22, derives from the fact that it was celebrated seven weeks
after Passover (see Lev 23:15-16; Deut 16:9-10). It was actually
celebrated on the day after the seventh week, that is, on the fiftieth day (Lev 23:16). This explains how it became known in
Greek as Pentecost, a word which means 'fiftieth (day)'. The
feast is mentioned under this Greek name in the New Testament
in Acts 2:1; 20:16; 1 Cor 16:8.

The characteristic feature of the Feast of Weeks in ancient times was the offering of new grain to the Lord (Lev 23:16-17; Num 28:26). In Exod 34:22 it is called the festival of 'the first fruits of wheat harvest, and the festival of ingathering at the turn of the year'. It is clear, then, that the Feast of Weeks was originally an agricultural festival. It marked the end of the barley harvest and the beginning of the wheat harvest. Jews still retain this agricultural aspect of the feast by decorating their synagogues with plants, greenery and flowers for the festival. The Bible does not link the Feast of Weeks with any historical event in the history of Israel as it does for the other 'pilgrim festivals', Passover and Tabernacles.

Post-Biblical Times

In post-biblical times the Feast of Weeks underwent a radical transformation. The Mishnah (c. 200 CE) still regarded it as an agricultural celebration, and it described how the people from the different towns of Israel brought offerings of fresh figs and grapes in joyful procession to Jerusalem to celebrate the festival. This, however, refers back to a time before the destruction of the Temple (70 CE) when people came from many lands to celebrate the Feast of Weeks (Pentecost) in Jerusalem (see Acts 2:1-13). But when the first-fruits of the harvest could no longer be offered in the Temple the agricultural aspect of the feast faded into the background.

The rabbis then gave a new meaning to the feast, and celebrated it as a memorial of the giving of the Torah on Mount Sinai. The liturgy for the day refers to the feast as 'The Feast of Weeks, the season of the Giving of our Law'. The Talmud states that one must rejoice on this feast because it is the day on which the Torah was given. The Bible does not tell us on what day the Torah was given on Sinai. But the rabbis, who believed that the Exodus took place on the fifteenth of Nisan, calculated that the revelation of Sinai took place on the sixth day of the Jewish month of Sivan, which corresponds to May/June in our calendar. Consequently the Feast of Weeks is celebrated on that date.

Traditional Customs

Unlike the feasts of Passover and Tabernacles, the Feast of Weeks has very few rituals associated with it. As noted above, synagogues are decorated with greenery and flowers on the occasion of the feast, and people adorn their homes in a similar manner. It is customary to partake of milk or milk products, or foods prepared with milk, and also to taste some honey, since the Torah, it is said, may be compared to honey (see Ps 19:10), and the rabbis, in the light of Is 55:1 ('Everyone who thirsts, come to the waters; ... Come, buy wine and milk without money'), said that the Torah is likened to these three liquids, water, wine and milk. Some traditional Jews observe the custom of spending the whole, or part, of the first night of the feast in the synagogue or in the study-hall studying Israel's sacred texts.

In modern times Reform Jews introduced the ceremony of Confirmation on the Feast of Weeks. In this ceremony boys and girls of sixteen or seventeen, who have followed a programme of religious instruction, commit themselves anew to Israel's Torah. Reconstructionist synagogues, and some Conservative communities, have also adopted this ceremony.

Since the Feast of Weeks celebrates the giving of the Law it is not surprising that the biblical account of the giving of the Torah (Exod 19:1-20:26) is read in the synagogue service for the feast day. During the reading of the Decalogue from this passage on this occasion, the congregation stands to show their respect for this central statement of Israel's Torah. The Book of Ruth is also read in the liturgy of the feast. This book is chosen because it treats of the two themes that are characteristic of the Feast of Weeks, namely, the grain harvest and the Torah. The story of Ruth is set against the background of the barley harvest (cf Ruth 1:22; 2:17, 23 etc.) and the wheat harvest (2:23), and Ruth is portrayed as one who left her own people and committed herself to the Torah of Israel (1:16).

CHAPTER SIX

The Sabbath

The Sabbath is the weekly day of rest which Jews observe from sunset on Friday evening to nightfall on Saturday. The word 'Sabbath' comes from the Hebrew *shabbath*, which means 'to rest'. This verb occurs at the very beginning of the Bible where we are told that God, having completed the work of creation, 'rested on the seventh day' (Gen 2:1-3). The third commandment of the Decalogue obliges all Israelites to refrain from work on the Sabbath just as God had rested on the seventh day (Exod 20:8-11). According to the version of the Decalogue which we find in Deuteronomy, the purpose of the institution of the Sabbath was to give a day of rest to all Israelites, to their slaves and to their animals (Deut 5:14). The story of the manna also teaches that the Israelites must refrain from work on the Sabbath. For five days God supplied sufficient manna for each day. On the sixth day he supplied a double portion, and on that day the people had to collect and prepare enough for two days, so that on the seventh day, the Sabbath, they would not have to work (Exod 16:1-30; especially vv 22-26).

During the biblical period the Sabbath was held in high esteem, and many biblical writers stressed the importance of observing it faithfully (see Amos 8:5; Is 58:13-14; Jer 17:19-27; Neh 13:14-22). Is 58:13-14 and Hosea 2:11 give us to understand that the Sabbath was a joyful day in ancient Israel, just as it is intended to be in Jewish communities today. In the second century BCE the Jews took the law of rest on the Sabbath so seriously that they allowed themselves to be slaughtered rather than take up arms against their aggressors on that day (1 Macc 2:29-38). Soon after that it was decided that Jews should defend themselves on the Sabbath against attackers (1 Macc 2:40-41).

In Post-Biblical Times

The Lord himself had established the Sabbath as a sign of the perpetual covenant between himself and Israel (Exod 31:16-17). In the course of history the observance of the Sabbath marked the Jews off as a distinct people. After the destruction of the Temple of Jerusalem in 70 CE, and with the cessation of its cult, the Sabbath became one of the principal distinguishing features of the Jewish community. Their day of rest set the Jews apart from their neighbours. The Romans, for example, could not understand the Jewish custom of refraining from work on their weekly holy day, and they regarded the weekly day of rest as a sign of indolence. Many Jewish writers, however, claim that it was the observance of the Sabbath laws and rituals that enabled the Jews to preserve their identity in a hostile environment down through the centuries.

So important was the observance of the Sabbath in the eyes of the rabbis that they could say that if Israel kept one Sabbath as it should be kept, the Messiah would come, because the Sabbath is equivalent to all the commandments. One who profanes the Sabbath publicly, the rabbis say, should be treated in the same way as an idolater. Conversely, one who observes the Sabbath according to its laws will have his/her sins forgiven, even if he/she had practised idolatry. The Sabbath was not only a day for spiritual exercises, but also a day for physical rest and enjoyment, and Jews were urged to celebrate it 'with food and drink and clean clothes, deriving physical enjoyment therefrom'. Even the poorest Jew should enjoy three meals on the Sabbath. The rabbis taught that on the Sabbath Jews are given an additional soul so that they can have a deeper appreciation of the spiritual dimension of life.

Sabbath Observances: 'You Shall Do No Work'

Exod 20:10; 23:12 and 34:21 and Deut 5:12-14 stipulate that the Israelites must refrain from work on the Sabbath. The Mishnah lists thirty-nine kinds of work that are forbidden on the Sabbath. Among these are ploughing, sowing, weeding crops, reaping,

baking, sewing, writing, lighting a fire etc. The rabbis discussed
each of these topics and established how the rules governing
them should be applied. Thus, for example, by the time of Jesus
'reaping' was taken to include even the gathering of a few ears
of corn (see Mk 2:23-24). Cooking food is forbidden, so that
meals must be prepared before the Sabbath and kept hot until
required. Since the Bible forbids the lighting of a fire on the
Sabbath (see Exod 35:3), traditional Sabbath law forbids the use
of electricity, which is taken to be a form of fire. Similarly, it is
forbidden to ride in cars, which produce energy through com-
bustion. One may not request a non-Jew to do work on the
Sabbath which is forbidden to a Jew. But a non-Jew may be
asked to do something that 'is required for health'. In cold climates lighting a fire to heat the home falls into this category.

However, in spite of the strict laws that forbade work on the
Sabbath, the prohibitions of the law can be disregarded whenever
life might be at stake. The rabbis stated the principle that 'the
duty of saving life supersedes the Sabbath laws. ... The Sabbath
is given to you but you are not surrendered to the Sabbath.' The
Christian reader will immediately notice the similarity between
this rabbinic text and the statement of Jesus as recorded in Mk
2:27. The biblical basis for the rabbinic principle of saving life on
the Sabbath is Lev 18:5: 'You shall keep my statutes and my ordinances; by doing so one shall live.' The rabbis interpreted this to
mean that one shall live by observing the commandments, but
one shall not die as a result of observing them.

Thus, for example, if a building falls on a person on the
Sabbath one must remove the debris to rescue him/her, even if
this means breaking the Sabbath laws. Everything possible must
be done to help a person who is ill. One may, for example, light a
fire to keep the patient warm, or one may light a lamp or candle
for his/her comfort. One may rescue an animal whose life is in
danger. See Mt 12:11. Whatever is required for national security
and well-being is allowed. Thus, soldiers may carry weapons,
members of the fire-brigade may drive trucks, hospital person-
nel may perform necessary tasks.

The Sabbath Limit

According to the story of the manna, the Lord, having commanded the Israelites to collect enough manna for two days on the sixth day, added the command, 'Do not leave your place on the seventh day' (see Exod 16:29). This command is the basis for the rabbinic stipulation that a Jew should not go beyond the 'Sabbath limit' on the Sabbath. The 'Sabbath limit' was the area extending 2,000 cubits, that is, a little over half a mile, in every direction around a town or village. In referring to 'a Sabbath day's journey' the author of Acts 1:12 had a journey within those limits in mind.

Celebrating the Sabbath

The Sabbath begins on Friday at sunset. A little before sunset the woman of the house lights the Sabbath candles while reciting the blessing:

> Blessed are you, O Lord our God, King of the universe, who has sanctified us by your commandments, and commanded us to kindle the Sabbath light.

Traditionally it has been only men and male children who attend the synagogue service on Friday evening. On their return from the synagogue, they find everything prepared for the Sabbath evening meal. A clean white cloth is placed on the table, and on it are placed the Sabbath loaves. These are two in number to commemorate the double portion of manna which the Israelites received in the desert on the eve of the Sabbath (Exod 16:22, 29). The loaves are covered with an embroidered napkin – symbolising the 'layer of dew' which covered the manna (Exod 16:13-15). The Sabbath bread, which is called *hallah*, is made of white flour and often shaped in the form of plaits. At least two candles are placed on the table, symbolising the two commandments, 'Remember the Sabbath day' (Exod 20:8) and 'Observe the Sabbath day' (Deut 5:12).

Just before sitting down to eat the Friday evening meal, the *Kiddush*, or 'sanctification', a formal blessing of the Sabbath, is pronounced over a glass of wine. This 'sanctification', or blessing, is in accordance with the Biblical command: 'Remember the sabbath day, to keep it holy' (Exod 20:8). Before the actual blessing the text of Gen 2:1-3, is usually read. This text states that God blessed the seventh day, hallowed it, and rested from the work of creation. Two blessings follow, one for the wine and the second for the Sabbath:

> Blessed are you, O Lord our God, King of the universe, who creates the fruit of the vine. Blessed are you, O Lord our God, King of the universe, who has sanctified us by your commandments and has taken pleasure in us, and in love and favour has given us your holy Sabbath as an inheritance, a memorial of creation, that day being the first of the holy convocations in remembrance of the departure from Egypt ...

A more tasty fare than usual is provided at the meal in order to add to the joy of the Sabbath. At the end of the meal the participants sing religious table songs, the central theme of which is the delight of the Sabbath. Finally, the Grace after meals is said. This, however, is much longer than our ordinary Christian Grace.

According to the rabbis three meals must be eaten on the Sabbath, one on Friday evening, and two on Saturday. In rabbinic times people usually ate only two meals a day, so that the added meal was a symbol of the festive spirit of the Sabbath.

The synagogue services on the Sabbath are longer than usual, but their mood is one of praise and thanksgiving. The Sabbath gives everyone leisure for prayer and study, and many men spend the afternoon in the synagogue studying Jewish religious literature and discussing religious matters in groups.

On the Sabbath, Jews greet each other with the salutation *Shabbat shalom*, 'the peace of the Sabbath'. They also like to refer to what they call 'the joy [or: delight] of the Sabbath' (see Is 58:13). Peace and joy are without doubt characteristics of the Jewish Sabbath. Free from the demands and the stress of the daily round of duties, worshipping and praying with the sacred texts and rites of the Jewish people, relaxing and enjoying good food in the intimacy of one's family or friends, the Jew experiences a sense of well-being that brings peace, relaxation and joy to the human spirit.

A prayer which is recited at the Afternoon Service for Sabbaths expresses the Jew's understanding and appreciation of the Sabbath as a gift from God, and as an observance that was dear to the Patriarchs:

You are One and your name is One, and who is like your people in Israel, a unique nation on earth? Glorious greatness and a crown of salvation, even the day of rest and holiness, you have given to your people – Abraham was glad, Isaac rejoiced, Jacob and his sons rested thereon – a rest vouchsafed in generous love, a true and faithful rest, a rest in peace and tranquility, in quietude and safety, a perfect rest wherein you delight. Let your children perceive and know that this their rest is from you, and by their rest may they hallow your name.

Havdalah

The Sabbath comes to a conclusion with a ceremony of blessing called 'Havdalah'. The Hebrew word *havdalah* means 'separating, distinguishing', and the ceremony of that name marks the separation of the holy Sabbath from the secular weekdays. It highlights Jews' understanding of the relationship between holiness and time. The ritual is performed by the head of the household after the evening prayer. A special candle made of at least two intertwining strands of wax, and producing several flames, is lit for the occasion. Blessings are pronounced over a cup of wine, over a box of spices, and over the lighted candle. The use of spices in this ritual has been variously explained. One popular explanation is that the sweet-smelling spices afford comfort to the Jews who grieve at the departure of the Sabbath. Holding the cup of wine in his right hand the head of the house says a final blessing, beginning with the following words which bring out the meaning of the *Havdalah* (separating) ceremony:

Blessed are you, O Lord our God, King of the universe, who makes a distinction between holy and profane, between light and darkness, between Israel and other nations, between the seventh day and the six working days.

The Kiddush

The Hebrew word *kiddush* means 'sanctification', and the ritual that is known by that name is a prayer of blessing that is recited over a cup of wine in the home or in the synagogue to sanctify the Sabbath or a festival. The basis for this ritual is the command 'Remember the Sabbath day, to keep it holy' (Exod 20:8). In Hebrew the verb 'to keep holy' is *kaddesh*, and from this we get the term *kiddush*. The *kiddush* is primarily a home ceremony. It is recited on the eve of the Sabbath, or of a festival, before the evening meal. On the eve of the Sabbath the *kiddush* focuses on the Sabbath as a commemoration of creation and of the Exodus. On festivals it expresses the characteristic feature of the celebration. The *kiddush* is often recited in the synagogue after the morning service on the Sabbath or on festivals. On these occasions it may be sponsored by an individual family that celebrates some special occasion, or by the congregation, and it takes on the nature of a social gathering.

The Kiddush for Sabbath Evening begins with the recitation of Gen 1:31 – 2:3 and continues as follows:

Blessed are you, O Lord our God, King of the universe, who creates the fruit of the vine.

Blessed are you, O Lord our God, King of the universe, who has sanctified us by your commandments and has taken pleasure in us, and in love and favour has given us your holy Sabbath as an inheritance, a memorial of the creation, that day being the first of the holy convocations, in remembrance of the departure from Egypt. For you have chosen us and sanctified us above all nations, and in love and favour have given us your holy Sabbath as an inheritance. Blessed are you, O Lord, who sanctifies the Sabbath.

CHAPTER SEVEN

Pilgrimage in Judaism

When the Israelites were still in Egypt, Moses requested Pharaoh to allow them to go to worship the Lord in the wilderness (Exod 7:16). Pharaoh did in fact give them permission to go, and Moses replied that he and all the people would set out on the pilgrimage. He explained to Pharaoh that 'we have the Lord's festival to celebrate' (10:9). The Hebrew word which is here translated as 'festival' is *hag*, which corresponds to the Arabic word *hajj*, a term used to refer to the pilgrimage to Mecca which every Muslim must make once in a lifetime.

When they settled in their own land, the Israelites continued to go on pilgrimage, and they used to journey to well-known shrines to worship the Lord. Elkanah, for example, accompanied by his wives, 'used to go up year by year from his town to worship' at Shiloh (see 1 Sam 1:1-7). Bethel, where Abraham had built an altar (see Gen 12:7), became an important cult centre (see e.g. Judg 20: 26-28). But when, in about 960 BCE, Solomon built the Temple in Jerusalem (see 1 Kings 6) that city became the main centre of Israelite worship, and its elaborate sacrificial system attracted pilgrims from all over Israel. After about 600 BCE the duty of offering sacrifices to the Lord on the occasion of the three Pilgrim Festivals (see Important Jewish Festivals) could be fulfilled only in Jerusalem which was regarded as the place where God had chosen to dwell (see Deut 12:5, 11, 14). After that date all other sanctuaries ceased to be places where legitimate sacrifices could be offered, and Jerusalem, 'the city of God', the place where the Most High dwelt (see Ps 46:4), became the focal point of Israelite religion.

Longing for the House of the Lord

Pilgrimage to Jerusalem is a recurring theme in the psalms. The author of Ps 84 declares that his soul longs for the courts of the Temple in Jerusalem where the Lord of hosts dwells (vv 1-2). The poet declares blessed those who keep 'the highways to Zion' in mind (v 5), that is, those who have set their hearts on a pilgrimage to the holy city. Ps 48 calls Jerusalem 'the city of God' (v 1) and it describes the Temple as the place where the people can ponder the Lord's steadfast love (v 9). It was a joy and a privilege for the Israelite to be able to accept the invitation: 'Walk about Zion, go all around it, count its towers, consider well its ramparts; go through its citadels' (Ps 48:12-13). The Bible gives the title 'Song of Ascents' to each of the psalms from Ps 120 to Ps 134. It is very probable that these psalms were sung by pilgrims as they 'ascended' to Jerusalem, the city which the Lord chose as his own and which he desired for his habitation (see Ps 132:13). Ps 122 in particular expresses the joy of the pilgrim who has arrived in the house of the Lord, and it captures the religious emotion felt by the pious Israelite who stood in awe in the majestic courts of the Temple (verses 1-2).

The Pilgrim Festivals

Although the Bible states that all male Jews must 'appear before the Lord', three times each year (see Exod 23:17) this injunction was not taken to mean that every male Jew must go on pilgrimage three times each year. Later Jewish literature shows that some Jews, especially those who lived near the Holy city, went up to Jerusalem every year, while others made the journey once in several years, or even once in a lifetime. Lk 2:41 informs us that every year the parents of Jesus went to Jerusalem for the festival of Passover, and that at least on one occasion Jesus accompanied them (vv 42-51). From John's gospel we learn that Jesus made several visits to Jerusalem (see Jn 2:13; 5:1; 7:10; 12:12). The story of the passion of Jesus is set in the context of the Passover festival in Jerusalem (see Mt 26:2.17-19).

The Jewish historian Josephus, who wrote in about the year

90 CE, claims that there would have been nearly three million people in Jerusalem for the Passover celebration. This figure would seem to be a wild exaggeration, but it does allow us to conclude that vast throngs crowded the holy city for the feast. The Acts of the Apostles states that at the feast of Pentecost 'there were devout Jews from every nation under heaven living in Jerusalem', and it mentions peoples from Mesopotamia to Rome who were represented at the festival celebrations at the central shrine of Judaism (Acts 2:1-11). Philo, a Jewish philosopher who lived in Alexandria at the time of Jesus, states that 'countless multitudes from countless cities come to the Temple at every festival, some by land and some by sea, from east and west, from north and south'.

Today's Jewish Pilgrims

In the centuries following the destruction of Jerusalem in 70 CE we have scarcely any information about Jewish pilgrims to the Holy Land. However, after the Arab conquest of Palestine in 640 the flow of pilgrims seems to have begun again, and ever since then pious Jews have gone to visit the places that were so well known to them from their Bible. Jerusalem, the city of David and the site of the once glorious Temple, was the focal point of their journey. For centuries pious Jews have prayed at the place they know as the 'Western Wall', and which many in Europe call the 'Wailing Wall'. Although this wall was not part of the ancient Temple, but part of the supporting wall of the Temple Mount, it has become the most sacred spot in the Jewish religious consciousness, and Jewish pilgrims constantly make their way there to mourn for the destruction of the Temple. Hence the name 'the Wailing Wall'. Praying at the Western Wall is the high point of a Jew's pilgrimage to the Holy Land.

Besides Jerusalem there are many holy places in Israel that have attracted, and continue to attract Jewish pilgrims. Hebron, about 35 km south of Jerusalem, is venerated as the burial place of the patriarchs, and it has always been a place of pilgrimage for Jews, Christians and Muslims. The alleged tomb of Rachel,

Jacob's wife, at Mamre near Bethlehem, is also a centre of Jewish pilgrimage. The tombs of great Jewish teachers of the past are also venerated as holy places and frequented by pilgrims. So, for example, Orthodox Jews gather annually at Meiron in Galilee around the tomb of Rabbi Shimon ben Johai, a famous rabbi of the second century CE.

CHAPTER EIGHT

The Synagogue

We do not know when or where the synagogue first came into being, and there are many unanswered questions about its development over the centuries. But no one challenges the view that after the destruction of the Second Temple (70 CE) the synagogue became the central institution in the religious and social life of Jewish communities in the Land of Israel and in the Diaspora. Until that date, the Temple, and not the synagogue, served as the focus of religious life in the land of Israel, and the pilgrim feasts brought crowds from all over the Diaspora to worship in the sanctuary in Jerusalem (cf Acts 2:1-11). This was the place where God dwelt among his people, and where sacrifice was offered to him in order to make atonement for the sins of the people (cf e.g. Deut 12:4-7, 14; Lev 4:13-35, esp. 20, 26, 31, 35). Sirach 50:5-21 expresses the people's reverence for the High Priest and their love of the liturgy over which he presided.

One opinion about the beginnings of the Synagogue is that it originated during the Babylonian Exile that followed the destruction of Jerusalem in 586 BCE. The exiles in Babylon gathered, it is claimed, to read or hear their scriptures and to worship. It is true that in the Exile the circumstances favoured the establishment of an institution where the Jews could recall their traditions and reflect on their sacred texts. But we have no direct proof that this actually happened. Others maintain that the synagogue was a development of fifth century Palestine. They appeal to the ceremony described in Neh 8:1-8, a ceremony which involved the reading and exposition of the scriptures. Others still say that the synagogue originated only with the rise of Pharisaism, i.e. in the second century BCE. Still others propose the view that the synagogue came into being only in the late second or early first century BCE. So the scholars differ, and questions remain, so that we cannot say with any confidence when the synagogue first became a prominent feature of Jewish community life. But there is a consensus that before the Destruction of the Temple in 70 CE the primary function of the synagogue was not religious. It was the centre of Jewish communal life, serving as a community centre where matters of public interest were discussed and where court proceedings took place, and as a setting for varied religious, educational and social activities, both in Israel and in the Diaspora.

'Synagogue' is a Greek word, the basic meaning of which is 'assembly', and it is used a few times in the New Testament with this meaning (e.g. Acts 13:43; Rev 2:9; 3:9). A secondary meaning of the word is 'place of assembly', and it occurs in this sense about sixty times in the New Testament (e.g. Mt 4:23; 6:2). The most common Hebrew term for the synagogue, *beth ha-kenesset*, also means 'place of assembly'.

However, in our earliest surviving references to what we call the 'synagogue', the Greek term used means 'house of prayer'. These references occur in inscriptions that were found in Egypt in the third century BCE. 'House of prayer' rather than 'synagogue' was in fact the term most commonly employed outside Palestine. Although the term 'house of prayer' indicates that the synagogue served mainly as a place of worship, other inscriptions show that in Egypt, as elsewhere, the building in question served as a kind of social centre where community matters could be discussed and where religious education could take place.

Unambiguous Evidence

The earliest clear archaeological evidence we have for the existence of a synagogue in Israel is found in what is known as the Theodotus Synagogue Inscription, which was found in a rubbish heap at the bottom of a cistern in Jerusalem. Although it has often been repeated that the inscription can be dated to before 70

CE, many responsible scholars dispute this, and claim that the inscription comes from the second half of the second century CE. The inscription, which was written in Greek, reads as follows:

> Theodotus, son of Vettanos, priest and synagogue leader … built this synagogue for the purpose of the reading of the Law and for the instruction of the commandments of the Law, the hostel and guest rooms, and the baths for foreigners who need them ….

We learn several things about a synagogue from this inscription:

- The reading of the Torah, probably in a liturgical service, took place there.
- The synagogue served as a kind of school in which people received 'the instruction of the commandments of the Law'. Down through the centuries, right up to the present day, the synagogue has been a centre of education and instruction. This is indicated by the fact that one of the more popular Hebrew names for the syangogue is *beth midrash*, 'house of study'. The word for synagogue in Yiddish is *shul* (school).
- The mention of 'the hostel and guest rooms' shows that the synagogue had a social function and served the needs of travellers and pilgrims.
- There is no mention of prayer; but this may be due to the fact that in Jerusalem the Temple was the place of prayer.
- We may also note that the term 'synagogue leader' (*archisynagogos*) which occurs in the inscription is also found in the New Testament, e.g. Mk 5:22, 35-36; Lk 8:41; Acts 13:15.

The many references to synagogues which we find in the New Testament (e.g. Mk 1:21; Mt 13:54; Acts 6:9) prove that synagogues were common in Palestine, and indeed in the whole Roman Empire (see e.g. Acts 14:1; 17:1), in the first century CE. It is clear from these references that the synagogue was not a new institution, but something that had been long established in Palestine and in the Diaspora. The Jewish historian Josephus, who wrote at the end of the first century CE, also mentions syna-

gogues in Palestine at this time. From Philo, a Jewish philosopher who lived in Alexandria at the time of Jesus, we learn that
there were synagogues in Alexandria and in Rome in his time.
Many of these 'synagogues' may have been rooms in private
houses, and they would have served as places of prayer and
scripture reading, and as meeting places where the affairs of the
Jewish community were discussed.

Early Development

We know from New Testament texts like Lk 4:16-27 and Acts
13:14-43, as well as from Josephus and Philo, that the reading of
the scriptures and preaching took place in synagogues in the
first century CE. These texts also show that the reading and
preaching were done by ordinary members of the congregations. The passage from Luke just mentioned refers to several
formalities that were to become characteristic of the synagogue
service: standing up to read the scriptures (Lk 4:16); the attendant handing the scroll of the scriptures (vv 17, 20); finding the
place at which to begin the reading (v 17), a place that must have
been fixed beforehand; returning the scroll to the attendant (v
20); sitting down to explain the scriptures in terms that were relevant to those present (vv 20-22).

Since most of the congregation in a Palestinian synagogue in
New Testament times would not have understood the Bible in
Hebrew, the reading of the scriptures was accompanied by a
translation into Aramaic, the vernacular of the day in Palestine.
It is very probable that prayer formed part of the synagogue service at least on the Sabbath, on fast days and on feastdays. By the
end of the second century CE the basic constituents of the synagogue services had been established, although new elements
continued to be added in later times and in different places.
Standardised liturgical texts appeared only in the ninth and tenth
centuries. Today there is a variety of synagogue Prayer Books in
circulation in the different branches of Judaism. All these books
follow essentially the same structure while differing considerably in content and in the amount of the text that is in Hebrew.

The Building and its Furnishings

As already stated, the earliest synagogues served a variety of functions, secular and religious. Private houses, or even larger rooms in a house, could serve as synagogues. By the beginning of the third century, however, synagogues were taking on a definite religious character. Torah reading and religious instruction became the dominant elements in synagogue activities, and secular affairs received less attention. Buildings were now being constructed and furnished to suit the new situation. In the early centuries the ark or Torah shrine, which contained the Torah scrolls, was not permanently housed in the synagogue, but was carried or wheeled in when required. By the beginning of the fourth century it was placed in an apse in the wall facing Jerusalem. This meant that when people prayed facing the ark they were also facing the Holy City. The Torah shrine was adorned with richly decorated curtains or drapes. In the centre of the sanctuary there was a platform on which the person who read the scriptures, or the prayer-leader, stood. Nowadays, the platform may be placed in front of the ark. The platform is usually referred to as the *bimah*, which is actually the Greek word for 'elevated place, platform'.

A lamp, known as 'the eternal lamp', or, to use its Hebrew name, *ner tamid*, burned perpetually in front of the ark which contained the Torah scrolls. It usually hung from the ceiling. Traditionally, it consisted of a wick burning in olive oil, but nowadays it is usually an electric light. The lamp was seen as a reminder of the light that burned continually in the Temple (Exod 27:20; Lev 24:2). According to the rabbis the perpetual lamp symbolises the Shekinah, the Divine Presence that dwells with Israel.

Some early synagogues were decorated with geometric figures, with ritual objects such as the menorah and the shofar, or with plants and animals. Later, in contravention of such texts as Lev 26:1, human images appeared in synagogue decorations. In present-day Syria, in the ruins of the famous synagogue in Dura Europas on the Euphrates – which was destroyed in 256 CE and excavated in the years 1928-1932 – many beautiful frescoes depict biblical scenes in which Moses, Aaron, Jacob, David etc were found. From the beginning of the sixth century the tendency to avoid human figures reasserted itself.

Although the rabbis stated that synagogues should be built only at the highest point of the town, this ideal could not be put into practice in medieval Europe since the ecclesiastical authorities stipulated that synagogues should be lower than Christian places of worship. From about 1600 onwards European Jews began to build more elaborate synagogues which were influenced by local architectural tastes. The Orthodox, however, even to this day, prefer smaller, more intimate synagogues.

In modern times a great variety of architectural styles are employed in the building of synagogues. In America, for example, the synagogue complex incorporates the synagogue proper as well as classrooms, social centres that provide a number of community services, and leisure facilities. The synagogue is therefore a kind of 'Jewish centre' which promotes the religious, cultural and social life of the Jewish community, and fosters a sense of Jewish identity and togetherness.

Women in the Synagogue

Texts like Acts 16:13-14; 17:1-4, show that women attended the synagogue in ancient times, and this is confirmed by statements in the Talmud. But it seems that women did not play any kind of liturgical role in the synagogue services. The rabbis stipulated that although, in principle, women can be called to read the scriptures publicly in the synagogue, they should not, 'out of respect for the congregation', be called to do so. This rabbinic stipulation may be compared with Paul's statement in 1 Cor 14:34-35.

Neither literary texts nor the findings of archaeology give a clear answer to the question whether or not women were seated separately from men in the ancient synagogues. One scholarly view is that in the early Christian centuries men and women usually occupied different parts of the synagogue. Sometimes the women may have been seated in a gallery, while at other times they may have had their place in the same general area as the men, but separate from them. Sometime during the early Middle Ages the practice of separate seating for the different sexes became customary. By the eleventh century the *mehitzah*, 'partition', was introduced. This was usually a kind of screen, made of lattice work, which was placed between the men who were seated in front and the women who sat in the rear. Most European synagogues of the Middle Ages had a women's gallery which made the separation between them and the men more marked. The Reform movement in Germany in the early nineteenth century abolished the *mehitzah* and the gallery, putting an end to the segregation of the sexes. In most Conservative synagogues this is also the case, while Orthodox communities still defend the retention of the gallery.

Synagogue Organisation

It seems that in the first two Christian centuries the rabbis were not very involved in the life of the synagogue. They certainly did not hold positions of control, and very little is known about their role in the shaping of the synagogue worship. It was the ordinary members of the Jewish community, or their chosen leaders, who controlled synagogue matters. It was they who hired and dismissed the synagogue functionaries.

Stories from the Talmud and from other sources show that one person could perform many functions in the community. One such story tells how, in about the year 200 CE, the leaders of a particular community requested a certain Rabbi Judah to send them a man who could serve as 'preacher, judge, hazzan, teacher of Bible and Oral Law, and who would attend to all our needs'.

The synagogue official most frequently mentioned in the New Testament, in synagogue inscriptions, in rabbinic texts and elsewhere is the 'synagogue leader'. As mentioned above we find reference to this functionary in the Theodotus Synagogue Inscription and in the New Testament. In spite of the many references we have to the 'synagogue leader' we have no clear picture of what his role was. It is clear that he was responsible for the organisation of the religious services in the synagogue, appointing readers and preachers (see Acts 13:15) and ensuring that nothing improper took place in the synagogue (see Lk 13:14). But it seems that his role extended beyond liturgical matters, and that he was responsible for the financial affairs of the synagogue, and that he held a leadership role in the Jewish community in general.

The cantor who sings at the services in the synagogue is called the *hazzan*. The *hazzan* as a synagogue functionary is known to us from the early Christian centuries. But in those times he performed a variety of tasks – especially in small communities. He sometimes chose the people who would read the Torah, a task which he shared with the 'synagogue leader'. He brought out the Torah scrolls for the readings, told the reader where to begin, led the people in the recitation of certain prayers. He also blew the shofar to announce the beginning of Sabbath and festivals. In some communities he also taught children. From about 600 on, the *hazzan*'s role as organiser and leader of the liturgical service and as cantor became more important. Since about 1800 the cantor's role became more like that of a professional singer in the synagogue. In recent times several schools for the training of cantors, men and women, have been established in America and elsewhere.

In Orthodox communities the rabbi does not usually lead the liturgical celebration, although he is expected to give a sermon on certain feastdays. In Reform and Conservative synagogues the rabbi regularly leads the service and preaches. He/she also officiates at weddings and funerals, acts as an interpreter of the Torah and takes responsibility for the religious education of the Jewish community.

A Quorum

A quorum of ten adult males, aged thirteen or over, was required before a public synagogue service could take place. This quorum was called a *minyan*, a Hebrew word which means 'number'. Traditionally women could not be counted as members of the *minyan*. Reform, Conservative and Reconstructionist communities have abandoned this position, and they allow women to form part of the minimum quorum of ten. This is hardly surprising since women have been ordained as rabbis in each of these branches of Judaism. A group that forms a *minyan* may hold a religious service anywhere, and they need no synagogue building. Neither do they need a rabbi or other official to lead them.

A Holy Place

The rabbis expected a great measure of respect for the synagogue, and they laid down certain rules of conduct for those who enter it: synagogues must not be treated disrespectfully; no frivolous conduct is allowed in them; it is forbidden to eat or drink in them; one should not stroll about in them, nor go into them in summer to escape the heat or in the rainy season to escape the rain; one should not deliver a private funeral address [one not attended by the general public] in them. But it is right to read the scriptures in them and to repeat Mishnah and to deliver public funeral addresses.

The Menorah

The Menorah, or seven-branched lampstand is probably the most popular of all Jewish symbols. According to the Bible the menorah was an important part of the furniture of the Tabernacle in the wilderness. From the description in Exod 25:31-40 we learn that it consisted of six branches, three on each side, curving upwards from a shaft which carried the central light. According to 1 Kings 7:49 there were ten menoroth (plural of menorah) in Solomon's Temple in Jerusalem.

According to Jewish Law it was forbidden to have a replica of the menorah outside the Temple. But fragments of actual menoroth have been found in the ruins of many ancient synagogues. In modern times too the menorah often features as a decorative element in the synagogue, appearing in metal representations, in paintings on synagogue walls, in stained glass windows, and in mosaics. It frequently figures as a decorative motif on books, on ornamental objects and on jewellery. The 'menorah' which Jews light in their homes during the feast of Hanukkah (see above, pp 70, 72) is usually referred to as a *hannukiyah*, and it has eight branches, one for each night of the feast.

CHAPTER NINE

The Shema and its Blessings

The liturgical unit known as 'The Shema and its Blessings' is composed of three passages from the Pentateuch (Deut 6:4-9; 11:13-21; Num 15:37-41) which are surrounded by a number of blessings. In the Hebrew text the opening word of the first of these scripture passages is *Shema*, which means 'Hear, [O Israel]', and it is this word that has given its name to the whole liturgical formula. The command – which is also contained in the first of the three texts just referred to – that the Israelites should keep these words in mind when they lie down and when they rise (Deut 6:7) is the basis for the custom of reciting the Shema in the morning and in the evening. In the morning the scripture texts are preceded by two blessings and followed by one, and in the evening they are preceded by two blessings and followed by two. The chart overleaf illustrates this layout.

The first prayer, 'Creator of Light', that precedes the morning Shema reads as follows:

> Blessed are you, O Lord our God, King of the universe, who forms light and creates darkness, you make peace and create all things. In your mercy you give light to the earth, and in your goodness you renew the creation every day continually. How manifold are your works, O Lord! In wisdom you have made them all. The earth is full of your gifts. ... The blessed God, great in knowledge, prepared and formed the rays of the sun. ... May you be blessed, O Lord our God, for the excellency of your handiwork, and for the bright luminaries you have made. ... O cause a new light to shine upon Zion, and may we all be worthy soon to enjoy its brightness. Blessed are you, O Lord, Creator of the luminaries.

Morning Blessings	Theme of Blessings	Evening Blessings
(1) Creator of Light: thanks God for the sunrise and for the miracles of creation.	CREATION – LIGHT	(1) Who brings Evening: praises God as the Creator of night.
(2) With abounding love: thanks God for his love for Israel. This love was made manifest when God gave the gift of the Law on Mount Sinai.	REVELATION	(2) With everlasting love: expresses the idea that since God in his love has given the Law to Israel, the Jews must meditate on it day and night.
	THE SHEMA Deut 6:4-9; 11:13-21; Num 15:37-41	
3) True and firm: a blessing in three parts proclaims God's redemptive acts in the past, and his continued saving presence.	REDEMPTION	3) True and trustworthy: celebrates the saving event of the Exodus. (4) Night prayer: 'Cause us, O Lord our God, to lie down in peace, and raise us up, O our King unto life ...'

Origin of the Shema

According to the Mishnah, the priests in the Temple (therefore before 70 CE) every day recited a blessing, the Ten Command-ments, and the Shema, and they concluded with another bless-ing. However, since we do not have the wording of this Temple ritual we do not know how closely or otherwise the later syna-gogue practice corresponds to it. What we do know is that by the time the Mishnah was edited (c. 200 CE) the custom of reciting the Shema twice a day was well established, and that it consisted of the three scripture texts and the blessings referred to above.

A Profession of Faith

The Shema is not so much a prayer as a profession of faith, and Jewish tradition does not use the phrase 'praying the Shema', but rather 'reading the Shema'. The first biblical text in the Shema (Deut 6:4-9) is a declaration of Israel's monotheistic faith and a call to total allegiance to the one God. The second text (Deut 11:13-21) contains the promise of a reward for those who fulfil God's laws, and punishment for those who disobey them; it continues with a command to keep the revealed laws always in mind. The third reading (Num 15:37-41) treats of the wearing of ritual fringes, or tassels (Hebrew, *zizit*), which remind the wearer of the commandments, and of one's duty to overcome the evil inclinations of the heart.

The first of the blessings that precede the biblical texts in the Morning Prayer addresses God as 'King of the universe', and it declares that the ministering spirits, the angels, 'take upon themselves the yoke of the kingdom of heaven', that is, they recognise God as Lord and they obey his will. Jewish tradition states that the person who recites the Shema also proclaims the oneness of God, acknowledges his kingship and takes it upon himself or herself to observe the commandments (see Deut 6:4-6). Consequently the recitation of the Shema is frequently referred to as 'the acceptance of the yoke of the Kingdom of Heaven'.

The first blessing also refers to God as the One 'who forms light and darkness', 'who prepared and formed the rays of the sun', 'who renews creation every day', and 'who makes the great lights', namely, the sun, the moon and the stars (see Gen 1:16). It is obvious that these ideas are very appropriate in a morning prayer. The theme of the second blessing is revelation and the gift of the Law to Israel. The blessing that follows the biblical texts in the morning proclaims God to be the Redeemer who rescued the ancestors from Egypt, and who continues to answer the people's prayers when they cry out for help. The two blessings that precede the biblical texts in the Evening Prayer, and the first one that follows them, are similar in content to the corresponding morning blessings. The second blessing that follows the biblical texts in the evening is a prayer for peaceful rest and for safety from all harm during the night.

Reciting the Shema

In addition to reciting the Shema in the Morning and Evening Prayer pious Jews recite it again before going to bed. One should always give full attention to its recitation, and people often place the right hand over the eyes while reciting the first verse in order to help concentration. Women are not obliged to recite the Shema, but it is customary for them to do so. It is not necessary to recite the Shema in Hebrew. One fulfils one's obligation by reciting it in any language. The Shema, a profession of faith, was recited by Jewish martyrs as they faced death, and even today it is often recited by Jews on their deathbed.

CHAPTER TEN

The Eighteen Benedictions, or The Shemoneh Esreh

The *Shemoneh Esreh* is the chief prayer of Judaism, recited three times every day – morning, afternoon and evening – by every Israelite, including women, slaves and children. The term *Shemoneh Esreh*, which simply means 'eighteen', is used to refer to this prayer because it originally consisted of eighteen benedictions. There are nineteen benedictions in the contemporary version. The prayer is also known as *ha-Tefillah*, 'The Prayer', because it was regarded as the prayer *par excellence*, the main element of the Jewish daily prayer. It is also known as the *Amidah*, 'the standing (prayer)', because worshippers stand during its recitation.

It is generally agreed that the Eighteen Benedictions did not all come into existence at the same time. Many scholars hold that while the earliest forms of the prayer may date back to about 150 BCE, the fully developed form of eighteen benedictions was attained around 70-100 CE. Even after that, the wording of the different Benedictions remained fluid, and it was only sometime after the year 600 that the definitive versions were established and put to writing. Even modern versions of the Eighteen Benedictions can differ slightly in their wording in different blessings.

Reciting the Shemoneh Esreh
Since the *Shemoneh Esreh* is understood as a communal prayer, the plural 'we' is used even when it is recited by an individual. As mentioned earlier it must be recited standing, and the worshipper must face Jerusalem while reciting it. When it is recited with a congregation, the worshippers first recite it individually,

and, if there is a *minyan* present, it is then recited by the leader. Originally the repetition took place for the benefit of uneducated people who did not know the prayers.

Eighteen Benedictions are recited on weekdays, but on Sabbaths and festivals only seven are said. On these days the first three and the last three benedictions are the same as those said on weekdays, and between these two sets of three, one benediction, which expresses the character of the Sabbath or the holy day, is said.

The following is a translation of parts of the first three prayers which are clearly prayers of praise:

1. Blessed are you, O Lord our God and God of our fathers, God of Abraham, God of Isaac, and God of Jacob, the great, mighty and revered God, who bestows lovingkindness, and possesses all things; who remembers the pious deeds of the patriarchs, and in love will bring a redeemer to their children for your name's sake. O King, Helper, Saviour and Shield. Blessed are you, O Lord, the Shield of Abraham. You, O Lord, are mighty forever; you revive the dead, you are mighty to save. Blessed are you, O Lord.

2. O King, Helper, Saviour and Shield ... You sustain the living with lovingkindness, you revive the dead with great mercy, you support the falling, you heal the sick, you free the captive, you keep your word to those who sleep in the dust. Who is like you, Lord of mighty deeds, and who is comparable to you, O King, who causes death and restores to life, and who causes salvation to spring forth?

3. You are holy, and your name is holy, and the holy praise you daily. Blessed are you, O Lord, the holy God ...

The final benediction (no 19) reads as follows:

19. Grant peace, welfare, blessing, grace, lovingkindness and mercy unto us and unto all Israel your people. Bless us, our Father, all of us together, with the light of your countenance. ... And may it be good in your sight to bless your people Israel at all times and in every hour with your peace. Blessed are you, O Lord, who blesses your people Israel with peace.

The twelfth Benediction is known as 'the benediction of the heretics', but it is in reality a curse against heretics and against the enemies of Israel. The text has undergone many changes over the centuries. Some scholars claim that the Christians may have been the primary target of the original 'Benediction'. It reads as follows:

And for slanderers let there be no hope, and let all wickedness perish in a moment; let all your enemies be speedily cut off, and uproot and crush and cast down the insolent, speedily in our days. Blessed are you, O Lord, who crushes enemies and humbles the insolent.

CHAPTER ELEVEN

Dietary Laws

The observance of certain dietary laws has always been a distinguishing characteristic of the Jewish people. Food which is considered fit for consumption according to the Jewish dietary laws is said to be kosher, a word which simply means 'fit [for eating by Jews]'.

The dietary laws are firmly rooted in the Bible, especially in Lev 11:1-47 and Deut 14:3-21, which list the kinds of animals, fish, birds and insects that may or may not be eaten by the Israelites. Whatever may be eaten is regarded as 'clean', and anything else is considered 'unclean'. We cannot always identify all the living creatures that are mentioned in these chapters, and the reasons why a particular creature is permitted or forbidden is not always obvious. But certain things are clear. For example, among the animals that have divided hooves and chew the cud, and are therefore allowed as food (Lev 11:3), are cattle, sheep, goats and game of different kinds (see Deut 14:4). The pig is excluded because it does not chew the cud.

Lev 11:9-12 states the general principle that the only water creatures that may be eaten are those that have 'fins and scales'. No particular water creature is mentioned as forbidden or allowed, but rabbinic tradition has excluded all kinds of shellfish, such as lobsters, oysters and crabs.

Lev 11:13-19 lists twenty birds that may not be eaten. The identity of some of the birds mentioned in this list cannot be determined with confidence, but it seems that birds of prey – like the vulture, the raven and the hawk – are all regarded as unclean. Jews who wish to be sure that they do not transgress the dietary laws eat only domesticated birds that have been traditionally regarded as kosher, such as chicken, duck, goose, turkey and pigeon. Verses 21-22, which deals with 'winged insects', permit the eating of certain types of locust. In this context we might recall that John the Baptist lived on 'locusts and wild honey' (Mk 1:6).

Scholars have been unable to discover the criteria by which the biblical writers decided which animals may be eaten and which may not. Perhaps one of the guiding principles was that only those animals that were acceptable as sacrificial offerings in the Temple may be eaten. But whatever may be said of the principles that guided the biblical writers, the Bible itself declares that the food laws were imposed on the Israelites because they were called to be a holy people (Lev 11:44-45). Every aspect of life, including diet, must be governed by this call to holiness, and the observance of the dietary laws set the holy people of Israel apart from every other nation.

Slaughtering and Preparing

Even animals that are considered kosher may not be eaten unless certain rules are followed when slaughtering them and when preparing the meat. An animal, for example, that had received a mortal injury from wild beasts, and that was found before it died, could not be eaten (Exod 22:31). The rabbis developed this idea, and the Mishnah lists seventy kinds of injuries or defects that render an animal unfit for consumption by Jews. These injuries and defects may be external, but they may also be found in the internal organs, e.g. heart, lungs, liver etc. A qualified 'slaughterer' must perform the act of slaughtering in such a way as to avoid inflicting unnecessary pain on the animal. He must, for example, use a knife that is as sharp as possible, free from the slightest dent, and spotlessly clean. (It may be noted that some defenders of animal rights regard the Jewish way of slaughtering as cruel, since it does not allow animals to be stunned before they are killed.) Having slaughtered the animal the slaughterer must examine the carcass for possible defects that would render the meat non-kosher.

'You Shall Not Eat Blood'

The law stating that blood must not be consumed was obviously of fundamental importance for the biblical writers since it is repeated several times (e.g. Lev 3:17; 17:10-13; Deut 12:16). The principle on which this law is based is stated in Lev 17:11: 'the life of the flesh is in the blood'. When blood is shed, life is poured out with it. Since life is a gift from God, blood may be looked on as the bearer of this gift, and may not be consumed by human beings. Therefore the eating of meat with blood in it is not allowed, and Jews have always slaughtered animals or poultry in such a way as to drain off as much blood as possible. The slaughtered animal is hung head downwards in order to facilitate this process. The flesh is later soaked in lukewarm water, and then salted on all sides so that the salt may draw out the remaining blood.

Milk and Meat

Biblical scholars have failed to find a convincing explanation for the prohibition 'You shall not boil a kid in its mother's milk', which occurs three times in the Pentateuch (Exod 23:19; 34:26; Deut 14:21). But from this obscure text the rabbis derived the law which forbids the cooking or eating of milk and meat together. 'Milk' includes all dairy products, such as butter, cheese and cream. One may not eat 'milk' and meat at the same meal. So, for example, one may not take cheese or a dessert which contains any form of milk, or coffee with milk, after a meal at which meat was eaten. Some Jews allow an interval of six hours between the consumption of meat and the eating of dairy products. Others assert that an interval of three hours is sufficient. Still others maintain that one hour suffices. Meat may be eaten almost immediately after one has eaten dairy products, provided one rinses one's mouth thoroughly and eats a morsel of bread.

In order to ensure that there is no mixture of milk and meat, strict observers of the kosher laws use separate cooking utensils, dishes and cutlery for meat and dairy foods. They even wash these things in separate sinks, dry them with different cloths (preferably of different colours, so that they cannot be confused), and store them separately.

Food Prepared By Non-Jews

There are no explicit biblical commandments against eating the bread or drinking the wine of non-Jews. But there are in some texts indirect warnings against these practices. Daniel limited his diet to vegetables and water so that he would not have to partake of the food and wine which the king provided (Dan 1:8-16). When Judith decided to go into the tent of Holofernes she took with her 'a skin of wine and a flask of oil, and filled a bag with roasted grain, dried fig cakes, and fine bread' (Judith 10:5). These stories, and others like them, were intended to encourage Jews to avoid consuming food or drink that had been prepared by Gentiles. Some New Testament texts (see Acts 11:3; Gal 2:12) show that it was not customary for Jews and Gentiles to eat together at the time when the church was in its infancy.

Bread and Wine

The rabbis, who regarded bread as the staple diet of the people, forbade Jews to eat bread that had been made privately by a non-Jew. But they allowed them to eat bread made by a non-Jew who was a professional baker. The rabbis also forbade the drinking of gentile wine since it might have been offered to pagan gods. Even gentile wine that had no association with pagan worship was forbidden, since drinking wine with Gentiles might lead to greater social contacts with them and to intermarriage. For all religious ceremonies, e.g. kiddush on Sabbaths and Festivals, the Passover Seder, only Jewish wine is considered kosher.

Today there is great variety in the ways in which Jews observe the kosher laws. As already mentioned, more observant Jews keep vessels and cutlery used for meat dishes separate from those used for milk-based foods. Many Conservative Jews also keep meat and dairy dishes separate. Outside their homes some will eat only bread they have brought with them lest that provided by others may be non-kosher. At the other end of the spectrum are some Reform Jews who treat the kosher laws lightly, except the law that forbids the eating of pig meat.

CHAPTER TWELVE

Rituals and the Life Cycle

Like every society and culture, the Jewish community marks the life cycle of each Jew with rituals and ceremonies that are appropriate to the different stages in the individual's development as a human being. From the naming of an infant that has just begun life's journey to the funeral rites that mark a person's departure from this world, traditional ceremonies celebrate the social and religious changes that take place in the course of a person's life. However, the age old rituals that have been performed for centuries have proved insufficient in contemporary Jewish society. Due especially to the initiative of Jewish feminists, new religious rituals have been introduced in recent times to celebrate aspects of the female biological cycle that had been ignored in the rites and ceremonies that had been created over the centuries by males in male dominated Jewish communities. The result is that today rites of venerable antiquity combine with modern and contemporary ceremonies to express the spiritual, ethical and social values of the Jewish community, and to honour individuals who enter into a new stage of life and to affirm them in their new commitments.

CIRCUMCISION

The rite of circumcision, that is, the removal of the foreskin of the penis, was known to several peoples in the Ancient Middle East long before it was adopted by the Israelites. However, in Israel it acquired a new significance, and it became a distinctive sign of the cultural and religious identity of the Israelite people. So, for example, an Israelite woman could not marry an uncircumcised man (Gen 34:14-17; Judg 14:3), and there are many biblical texts which show that the Israelites despised uncircumcised peoples (e.g. 1 Sam 17:26, 36). In New Testament times circumcision was regarded as a sign that set the Jews apart from all other peoples. In Eph 2:11 the Jews are referred to as 'the circumcision' (NRSV), while the Gentiles are called 'the uncircumcision' (NRSV).

Religious Significance of Circumcision
According to Gen 17:12 God, speaking to Abraham, commanded that all male Israelites must be circumcised on the eighth day after birth. In the same chapter (vv 11 and 13) circumcision is described as 'a sign of the covenant' and as 'my covenant in your flesh'. To this day the Jews regard circumcision as a sign of the covenant between them and God, and they refer to it as 'the covenant of circumcision'. They see circumcision as the sign *par excellence* of the Jew's loyalty to God and to Judaism. A male who fails to observe the law of circumcision cuts himself off from his religious community (Gen 17:14) and ceases to be a member of the covenant people. Adult male non-Jews who wish to embrace the Jewish faith must undergo circumcision. However, circumcision has not only religious significance but also ethnic overtones, and it is observed by secular Jews who never participate in other religious ceremonies.

The Ritual of Circumcision
Circumcision must take place on the eighth day after the birth of a male child. If, however, the infant is very weak or sick the ritual is postponed until he is well. The circumcision of an infant is seen as a celebration for the whole community, and it usually takes place in the synagogue in the presence of a *minyan*. The one who performs the actual act of circumcising is known as a *mohel*. He must be an observant Jew who is familiar with the laws that are relevant to circumcision, and he must have received special training in the technique of circumcision. In some Reformed communities the rite is often performed by a doctor. A 'godmother' and 'godfather' have parts to play in the circumcision ritual.

The godmother takes the infant to the door of the synagogue where she hands him over to the godfather, who in turn hands him to the *mohel*. The latter places the child for a moment on the so-called 'Chair of Elijah'. This chair, which gets its name from the prophet Elijah, who is regarded as the patron of circumcision and the protector of Jewish infants, is left unoccupied except for the moment when the infant is placed on it. The child is taken from the chair and given to the godfather who holds him during the operation which then takes place. Immediately after the circumcision the father of the baby says the following blessing:

> Blessed are you, Lord God of all creation, who has sanctified us by your commandments and has commanded us to make our sons enter the covenant of our father Abraham.

The child is handed over to the father, and the *mohel* recites a blessing over a goblet of wine and pronounces a prayer for the welfare of the child.

In the course of this prayer the infant is given its name. That the custom of naming a child on the occasion of his circumcision was an ancient one is proved by the fact that it is mentioned in the New Testament (see Lk 1:59). The circumcision is followed by a festive meal at which special hymns are sung and special prayers said.

CELEBRATING THE BIRTH OF A GIRL

Traditionally the birth of a baby girl was celebrated by holding a naming ceremony in the synagogue, usually at the morning service on the Sabbath after the birth. The father was usually called up to read the Torah, and the child's Hebrew name was formally announced. A special prayer was said at this time for the well-being of the mother and the baby. Since the naming ceremony took place so soon after the birth, the mother would not normally be present.

In recent years more elaborate ceremonies to welcome a baby girl into the covenant community are being elaborated. Prompted by a desire for equality in ritual matters between the sexes, some congregations, or families within congregations, arrange home rituals to celebrate the birth. Such a celebration is called *simchat bat*, 'rejoicing for a daughter'. It may take place on the eighth day after the birth, as is the case with circumcision, or at another time. The mother of the baby recites a prayer of thanksgiving for a safe delivery, and other suitable prayers and readings are chosen. A reading about one of the famous women in Israel's history (Sarah, Deborah, Hannah etc) is an obvious choice for the occasion.

BAR MITZVAH

The Hebrew term *bar mitzvah* may be translated literally as 'son of the commandment'. In its basic meaning it refers to a boy who has reached the age of thirteen, and must therefore observe all the obligations of the Jewish religion. Nowadays, the term is commonly used to refer to the synagogue ceremony which marks a boy's reaching that age and that status. The Mishnah and the Talmud state explicitly that on reaching the age of thirteen a boy has attained legal maturity and is therefore obliged to observe the religious duties of a Jew. But there seems to have been no special rite to mark the occasion. It was only from the fourteenth or fifteenth century that a Bar Mitzvah ceremony became part of the synagogue service, and the elaborate celebrations associated with Bar Mitzvah today were unknown even a hundred years ago.

Nowadays the Bar Mitzvah ceremony takes place in the synagogue, usually during the Sabbath morning ceremony. At the time of the reading of the Torah the boy and his father are called to the reader's desk. The father says the blessing, 'Blessed be He who has freed me from the responsibility of this child', expressing the thought that the boy now takes on responsibility for his own actions. The boy is invited to read parts of the texts from the Torah scroll and from the prophets that are assigned for the day. He has prepared and rehearsed these readings for months under the guidance of a tutor. The boy is also invited to deliver an address to the congregation. At a weekday morning service, usually on the Thursday before his Bar Mitzvah ceremony, a boy puts on the *tefillin* for the first time, and from the actual day of the ceremony he is obliged to wear them at Morning Prayer. For some time previously he has learned the rather complicated rules for putting on these ritual objects. The presiding rabbi preaches a sermon in which he reminds the boy of his new privileges and duties. After his Bar Mitzvah a boy may be counted as a member of a *minyan*, or quorum of ten males that must be present before a liturgical service can take place.

After the ceremony the congregation shares in a festive kiddush, and the boy receives congratulations and presents from family and friends. Later the boy with his immediate family and their friends enjoy a banquet that marks the happy occasion.

BAT MITZVAH

Bat Mitzvah, literally, 'daughter of the commandment', is the status a girl attains when she reaches the age of twelve. On reaching that age a girl is considered an adult in Jewish law, and she is obliged to observe all the laws that are binding on Jewish women. Before the nineteenth century there is no mention of a ceremony that was associated with a girl's reaching maturity. In that century a German rabbi introduced a non-synagogal ceremony to mark the occasion, and the practice gradually spread to other European communities. In 1922 Bat Mitzvah was formally celebrated in a synagogue when Rabbi Mordechai Kaplan, founder of the Reconstructionist Movement, officiated at his daughter's Bat Mitzvah. By the 1960s, the ceremony was commonly accepted by Conservative Jews. Since the 1960s, it has gradually won a place in Reform communities, and it is now firmly established in almost all Reform synagogues. Some Ultra-Orthodox communities still refuse to adopt the Bat Mitzvah ceremony.

Since there is no established tradition about the Bat Mitzvah ritual there is great variety in the way in which it is celebrated in contemporary communities. Today, many non-Orthodox Jews celebrate Bat Mitzvah in the same way as a Bar Mitzvah. Other

Tefillin

The Tefillin are two cube-shaped leather boxes which are attached by leather straps, one to the forehead and one to the arm. They are worn by adult male Jews at the Morning Prayer on weekdays. Little scrolls on which the text of Exod 13:1-10; 13:11-16; Deut. 6:4-9 and 11:13-21 is written are placed in each of the two boxes. The practice of wearing tefillin is based on the fact that each of these texts prescribes that the word of God be written 'on your hand' and 'on your forehead' (literally: 'between your eyes'); see Exod 13:9, 16; Deut 6:8; 11:18. Understood metaphorically these prescriptions can be taken to mean that every action and every thought of the Israelite must be guided by the Law of God. In Jewish tradition, however, they have been taken literally, and the four passages mentioned have been placed in the tefillin.

In Mt 23:5, where the tefillin are mentioned, this Hebrew term is rendered in Greek as 'phylacteries'. Although this word is sometimes used in English to refer to the tefillin, English-speaking Jews tend to ignore it, preferring to use the Hebrew term without translation.

The rabbis have laid down very precise rules about the making of phylacteries. The parchment on which the biblical verses are written must be made from the skin of ritually clean animals, preferably that of a calf. The text must be written by hand, and by a trained scribe.

The phrase 'on your hand' mentioned above is taken to mean 'on your arm', and the box on the hand is placed on the left arm, above the elbow. The box 'before the eyes' is placed above the forehead. The four biblical texts, written on one piece of parchment, are placed in the box on the hand. In the box on the forehead there are four compartments in which four parchments are placed, one for each of the four texts. Detailed rules are also laid down for the putting on of the tefillin, and special benedictions are recited when they are being put on.

When a boy reaches the age of thirteen he is obliged to put on the tefillin. Today Orthodox and Conservative Jews wear tefillin at prayer, while Reform Jews generally do not consider them obligatory. The tefillin are not worn on the Sabbath or on Festivals. Since Sabbaths and festivals are themselves 'signs', it would be superfluous to wear tefillin which are also 'signs' (see Exod 13:9, 16; Deut 6:8; 11:18). Women are not obliged to wear tefillin, although in recent times some women do wear them at prayer.

non-Orthodox synagogues may have a less elaborate ceremony for girls than for boys. The ceremony usually takes place when a girl reaches the age of thirteen, rather than at twelve. Nowadays, many Orthodox synagogues celebrate Bat Mitzvah, but they do not allow girls to read the Torah. Other Orthodox communities may celebrate Bat Mitzvah in a special ceremony for women in the synagogue. As in the case of Bar Mitzvah, the ceremony is followed by a congregational party and by family celebrations.

MARRIAGE

For Jews, marriage is an institution that is of divine origin (see Gen 2:18), and every Jew considers herself or himself obliged to get married in order to fulfil the divine command 'be fruitful and multiply' (Gen 1:28). At the circumcision of a baby boy, those present pray that the child may one day 'enter into the Torah, marriage canopy, and into good deeds'. The Talmud teaches that 'Any man who has no wife is no proper man', and that 'Any man who has no wife lives without joy, without blessing, and without goodness.' At the same time the rabbis warn against entering into marriage rashly. They give the advice: 'Be quick in buying land; be deliberate in taking a wife.'

Marriage, as Jewish tradition understands it, is a sacred relationship. But it is also a contract, the terms of which are set out in a document known as the *ketubah*. We are told in the Book of Tobit, which was written about 200 BCE, that when Tobit married Rachel, her father 'wrote out a copy of a marriage contract, to the effect that he gave her to him as wife according to the decree of the law of Moses' (Tobit 7:13). According to Jewish law the *ketubah* spells out the responsibilities of the husband to his wife, and it is legally binding in Jewish law. It is prepared before the wedding, signed by the future husband and two witnesses, and given to the bride during the wedding ceremony. It is written in Aramaic, the language of Palestine at the time of Jesus and the early rabbis. The *ketubah* is really a statement of the obligations a husband accepts at marriage. Its main purpose is to ensure the economic security of a wife if her husband decides to divorce her, or if he dies before her. It has often been said that in a world where women's rights were very limited, the *ketubah* clearly asserted the rights of a Jewish woman within marriage. However, the marriage contract is not a purely legalistic document as one may gather from the following (or similar) lines that usually form part of it:

I faithfully promise that I will be a true husband to you, I will honour and cherish you, I will work for you, I will protect and support you, and I will provide everything that is necessary for your due sustenance, as it is fitting for a Jewish husband to do.

Since about the twelfth century, it has become customary to present the *ketubah* as a beautifully illuminated document, and married couples display it prominently in their homes.

Although the Bible gives us several examples of polygamous marriages, e.g. Sarah and Hagar (Gen 16); Hannah and Peninnah (1 Sam 1), polygamy was discouraged by the rabbis. Nevertheless, it was not formally outlawed until the tenth century when it was proscribed in Germany. However, the ban was ignored by Jews who lived in Muslim territories where polygamy was culturally acceptable. In 1951 polygamy was universally condemned by the Chief Rabbis of Israel.

In earlier times the actual marriage rite consisted of two separate ceremonies, betrothal, and the marriage proper which usually took place at a later date, possibly even a year later. (Christians are familiar with the concept of betrothal, since Luke [1:27] says that Mary was betrothed [NJB; NRSV: engaged] to Joseph.) Between the two ceremonies – betrothal and marriage – the intended bridegroom and bride did not live together, and sexual intercourse between them was forbidden. Since the early twelfth century the two ceremonies take place together. Marriage never takes place on the Sabbath.

The wedding ritual begins when the groom is led to the *huppah*, or wedding canopy by his father and mother. Similarly, the bride is taken to the *huppah* by her parents. The *huppah* may be erected anywhere, in a synagogue, in another building, or out in the open. It consists of a large *tallith*, or prayer shawl draped over four standing poles, or it may be a more elaborate structure. Since marriage is a civil ceremony, there must be someone present to conduct the proceedings, but not necessarily a rabbi. According to Jewish tradition the presence of a *minyan* is desirable, but not obligatory. The rabbi, or the person conducting the ceremony, recites a prayer over a glass of wine for God's blessing on the marriage, and the bride and groom sip the wine. This is followed by the most important part of the ritual, the placing of a ring on the bride's finger by the groom who recites the words: 'You are consecrated to me, through this ring, according to the religion of Moses and Israel.' By accepting the ring the bride gives her consent to the marriage. This part of the ceremony is essential for the validity of the marriage, and it must take place in the presence of two witnesses. In some Reform and Conservative congregations, the bride may also place a ring on the groom's finger and make her own statement of marital commitment. At this point in the ceremony, the *ketubah* is read, in Aramaic with a translation, or in translation only, a speech or sermon may be delivered, and prayers are said. The second part of the ceremony begins when the officiating person, takes a glass of wine and pronounces seven marriage blessings. The following lines from the last of these blessings reflect the joyful nature of the marriage ceremony:

Blessed are you, O Lord our God, King of the universe, who has created joy and gladness, bridegroom and bride, mirth and exultation, pleasure and delight, love, brotherhood, peace and fellowship. Soon O Lord, our God, may there be heard in the cities of Judah, and in the streets of Jerusalem, the voice of joy and gladness, the voice of the bridegroom and the voice of the bride ... Blessed are you, O Lord, who makes the bridegroom to rejoice with the bride.

There follows a ritual that is peculiar to a Jewish wedding. The groom is given a glass, covered in a white cloth, which he places on the ground and crushes with his heel. The origins of this rite are obscure, but one of the most popular explanations for it is

that it is a reminder of the destruction of Jerusalem, a tragedy
that cannot be forgotten even on the joyful occasion of a marriage. Following this ritual the newly weds are led to a room
where they are left alone for a short time. These moments of pri-
vacy symbolise the consummation of the marriage. When the
new husband and wife rejoin the guests, a festive meal takes
place, and the guests celebrate the joy of the new husband and
wife with music, song and dancing. The meal ends with a special
grace after meals, and with the repetition of the seven blessings
mentioned above.

DIVORCE

Judaism has always esteemed marriage and extolled the
blessedness of happy married life. Permanent union of man and
wife was the ideal (cf Gen 2:24), and marital fidelity was expected
(cf Mal 2:13-15; Sirach 9:8-9). At the same time Jewish authorities
have been aware that not all marriages are successful and
happy. The reality of divorce was already taken for granted by
the biblical writers (e.g. Lev 21:7; Deut 22:19, 29). Nevertheless,
the Bible gives no clear indications about the reasons that might
justify a divorce, and it lays down no detailed rules about actual
divorce procedures. It is true that Deut 24:1 allows a man to divorce his wife 'because he finds something objectionable about
her'. But the interpretation of this verse has been problematic. It
was debated by the rabbis at the time of Jesus (see Mt 19:3-9).
Shammai, a contemporary of Jesus, who almost always opted
for a strict interpretation of the biblical laws, maintained that
'something objectionable' meant some kind of immoral behaviour. Hillel, another contemporary, who generally adopted a
lenient interpretation, taught that 'something objectionable' included anything that displeased the husband, even burning his
food. As was usually the case, the rabbis followed Hillel's lenient interpretation. The Deuteronomy text to which we have just
referred states that a man must write 'a certificate (or: bill) of divorce', but it tells us nothing about what that document should
contain. Furthermore, this text, and biblical law in general, al-

lows only the husband to initiate a divorce. The wife does not have this right. If her mariage breaks down she depends on her husband to grant her a divorce.

The rabbis acknowledged that in certain circumstances a divorce may be the only solution to a difficult situation. However, they regarded it as a last resort. They state, for example, that 'For him who divorces the first wife, the very altar sheds tears. ... all things can be replaced, except the wife of one's youth. ... Only with one's first wife does one find pleasure.' Rabbinic scholars debated many aspects of divorce, and they drew up detailed and complex rules that must be observed in the arrangement of a divorce. A marriage is dissolved when a man gives his wife a bill of divorce in the presence of a rabbi. This document, which is commonly known by the Hebrew word *get*, is written mostly in Aramaic and in terms that are based on the laws of the Mishnah. It is witnessed by two males who are over the age of thirteen.

Since about the eleventh century, most Jews followed the ruling that a man cannot divorce his wife against her will. Besides, there are, according to Jewish law, many reasons why a wife, through the court, can compel her husband to grant a divorce. Such reasons are, for example, if he refuses to provide her with adequate support (food, clothing), if he denies her conjugal rights, if he physically or mentally abuses her. However, this Jewish legislation was effective only where and when the Jews formed a self-governing community. Only then could the Jewish courts imprison or otherwise penalise a recalcitrant husband who refused to give his wife a *get*.

As we have said, traditional Jewish law stipulates that only the granting of a *get* by the husband brings formal closure to a marriage relationship. Consequently, a civil divorce is not sufficient to dissolve a Jewish marriage. However, Reform Jews have decided to break with this traditional ruling. They do not press the issue of the *get*, and they regard couples who have got a civil divorce as divorced in the eyes of the religious authorities also. Conservative and Reconstructionist authorities have devised ways of declaring that a woman who has not received a *get* is free to remarry. In the Orthodox tradition a woman must receive a *get* in order to remarry.

NIDDAH

Niddah is the Hebrew word for a menstruating woman or the menstrual period. It is also the title of a long tractate in both the Mishnah and the Talmud that deals mainly with matters related to menstruation, childbirth and family purity. According to the Bible (see Lev 15:19) a woman is considered impure, or unclean, during her days of menstruation. We must keep in mind, however, that the words 'impure' or 'unclean' in this context have no moral connotation, and that they imply no negative judgement of women or of their sexual functions.

Jewish law forbids a husband to have sexual relations with his wife during the time of her menstrual period (Lev 18:19). The rabbis took this to be at least five days, to which they added a further seven days after the cessation of the menstrual flow (see Lev 15:19). It is customary for strictly observant Jewish partners to refrain from any physical contact at all during these twelve days.

At the completion of the twelve days (five plus seven days just mentioned) the wife immerses herself in a *mikveh*, a ritual bath, and after that she may resume normal marital relations with her husband. Reform Jews and Reconstructionists have generally abandoned the use of the *mikveh*, except, as part of the preparation of converts. Conservatives retain the *mikveh* in principle, but it is rarely used except for the immersion of converts. The Orthodox continue to observe the laws concerning *niddah* and immersion in the *mikveh*.

The *Mikveh*

The Hebrew word mikveh occurs in Lev 11:36 with the meaning 'a gathering of water' (see NJB 'stretches of water'). In rabbinic literature it refers to a body of water in which a person immersed himself or herself for the purpose of ritual purification. In biblical times there were several ways in which a person could become 'ritually unclean'. Touching a corpse or a leper, for example, rendered a person unclean. In such cases one would have to immerse oneself in a *mikveh*. Originally, this would have been a natural body of water, such as a river, lake or pond. In later times it was usually an artificial pool or bath. The rabbis laid down strict rules for the construction of a *mikveh*. It must contain at least 250 litres of water. The water must come directly from a river or spring, or from the rain; it must not be carried to the *mikveh* in any vessel. Traditionally there are seven steps, representing the six days of creation and the Sabbath, leading down to the water. Strict procedures must be followed in the construction, filling, heating and draining of the *mikveh*. It is obligatory to wash thoroughly before entering the *mikveh*. This shows that the purpose of immersing oneself in the *mikveh* is ritual purity, not bodily cleanliness. Today, the *mikveh* is most frequently used by women before they resume sexual relations with their husbands after menstruation.

DEATH, BURIAL AND MOURNING

In many Jewish communities the rites surrounding death, burial and mourning are essentially the same today as they were in the Talmudic period (3rd-6th century CE). This is not true of Reform Jews who have modified the traditional customs considerably.

As one might expect, Jews treat a dying person with care and concern, and they show great respect for the bodies of their dead. Every effort must be made to reduce the pain of a dying person, and such a person must never be left alone. One may even break the Sabbath in order to assist the sick. Since life belongs to God alone, all branches of Judaism strongly oppose euthanasia and assisted suicide.

A Jew who feels that death is approaching should recite a confession of his/her sins. The Jewish daily Prayer Book provides the following prayer for the occasion:

I acknowledge before you, O Lord my God, and God of my

fathers, that both my cure and my death are in your hands. May it be your will to send me a perfect healing. Yet if my death is fully determined by you, I will lovingly accept it from your hand. May my death be an atonement for all the sins, iniquities and transgressions of which I have been guilty before you. Grant unto me the abounding happiness that is treasured up for the righteous. Make known to me the path of life. In your presence is fullness of joy; at your right hand happiness for evermore.

On hearing that someone has died, a Jew is supposed to respond 'Blessed be the True Judge'. This response expresses one's acceptance of God's decrees, no matter how hard it may be to accept the death of the person in question. Once death has been confirmed the eyes and the mouth of the deceased are closed, preferably by a close family member, and the body is carefully placed on the floor. In the absence of close relatives these services may be performed by a member of the 'Holy Society' (see next paragraph). According to Jewish custom, the dead must be buried as soon as possible, usually within twenty-four hours. This period can be extended if some close relatives must come from far away. The corpse is not left alone at any time between death and burial. It is laid on the floor and covered, and candles are lit next to it. 'Watchers', who may be relatives or friends, stay with the body and recite psalms until the burial. Autopsies are regarded as a desecration of the body and they are discouraged. They may be permitted, however, when required by law, or when there is a hope that they may benefit other sick people. In Orthodox communities close family members tear their clothing and wear the torn garments for the first seven days of mourning. In other communities this custom may be replaced by the tearing of one's tie, or by the wearing on the lapel of a small black ribbon which is torn.

The preparation of the corpse for burial is entrusted to a burial society, known in Hebrew as the 'Holy Society'. Today, however this task may be performed by the staff of a funeral home. The 'Holy Society' is a group, usually volunteers, who can be called on when someone dies. The members of the group wash the body according to established ritual, and wrap it in a shroud of linen. The same kind of shroud is used for everyone who dies, irrespective of the person's status in the community. A man is also wrapped in his prayer shawl, the tassels of which are cut off as a sign that the man being buried is no longer obliged to fulfil the commandments. In the Diaspora a little earth from the Holy Land is sprinkled on the body. Traditionally, Jews were buried in the shroud without the use of a coffin. If a coffin is used it is a simple wooden box made without nails. Most Jews are strongly opposed to cremation, but Reform Jews allow it. Prayers are said in the home, or nowadays in a funeral home, before taking the body for burial. Prayers are again said in the cemetery, and a eulogy may also be delivered. Taking part in a funeral is considered a meritorious deed, a *mitzvah*.

Several different stages can be distinguished in the Jewish mourning process. In the period between death and burial, usually less than twenty-four hours, the closest relatives are freed from religious obligation so that they can give all their attention to preparations for the funeral. At this time a mourner should not drink wine, eat meat, or engage in marital relations. After the burial, close relatives or friends prepare a meal for the mourners. This meal traditionally consists of hard-boiled eggs and bread. The eggs, being circular, are a symbol of the cycle of life, death, life.

The next stage of mourning lasts seven days. During those days, the mourners – father or mother, spouse, sibling or child of the deceased – remain at home and sit on low stools. They do not shave, cut their hair, use cosmetics, or have marital relations. They do not go to work. After the first three days, however, those who must go to work may do so. Friends and neighbours join the mourners at home to form a *minyan*, the required number of persons to recite the Kaddish, which cannot be recited without a *minyan*.

When seven days are complete a new stage of mourning begins, a stage that lasts until the thirtieth after the burial. During this time the mourners do not attend festive celebrations, including weddings and Bar Mitzvah, and do not frequent places of entertainment.

Children mourn a parent for a year after the burial. During this time, mourners avoid parties and celebrations, and they do not go to the theatre or to concerts. For eleven months, starting at the time of burial, the son, and nowadays the daughter also, of the deceased recites the mourner's Kaddish every day. There is a curious bit of reasoning behind the practice of reciting the Kaddish for eleven months rather than for a whole year. According to tradition, the truly wicked are punished in Gehenna for their sins for a period of twelve months after their death. This is the maximum period of punishment that God imposes. Since no one wishes to imply that a parent was so wicked as to have deserved the maximum twelve month's punishment, the custom of reciting the Kaddish for only eleven months established itself. It is customary to erect a tombstone on a person's grave on the first anniversary of his or her death.

The anniversary of a person's death is commemorated every year by close family members. They attend the synagogue service, and the eldest son, if capable of doing so, leads the prayer. The mourners join the community in the recitation of the Kaddish. It is also customary to light a candle for twenty-four hours in the home on the occasion of the anniversary.

JEWISH THOUGHTS ON LIFE AND DEATH

This world is like an antechamber before the world to come. Get ready in the antechamber, so that you can go into the Great Hall.

**

Consider three things and you will not fall into transgression:
    Know what is above you:
    An eye which sees you,
    an ear which hears,
    and all your actions are written down in a book.

The Kaddish

The Aramaic word *Kaddish* means 'sanctification', and the prayer in Aramaic which is known as the 'Kaddish' is a doxology, a prayer of praise. It begins with a prayer for the glorification and sanctification of the name of God, and it continues with an expression of longing for the establishment of his kingdom and for the coming of the Messiah. It is recited several times during the daily synagogue services, at the end of each of the main sections of the service. Although an elementary form of the prayer existed in the first century CE, it reached its present formulation only in the eighth or ninth century. It became part of the synagogue worship from about the sixth century.

Since the thirteenth century it has become the prayer of mourners even though it contains no reference to death. It is also recited in the cemetery when a body is being interred, and on the anniversary of the death of a loved one. It has been traditional for a bereaved son to recite the Kaddish for a deceased parent for a period of eleven months after the death. Nowadays some bereaved daughters also observe this custom. The Kaddish can only be recited when there is a *minyan* present.

The 'Our Father', the prayer formula which Jesus taught his disciples (see Mt 6:8-13) and which has become the basic Christian prayer, borrowed elements from the Kaddish as one can see from the following lines from that Jewish prayer:

Magnified and hallowed be the name of God in the world he created according to his will. May his kingdom come in your lives and in your days, and in the whole house of Israel. And let us say: Amen.

CHAPTER THIRTEEN

Judaism and Christianity
A Troubled History

Christians readily acknowledge that Jesus and his earliest disciples were Jews and that Christianity was born from Judaism. They are aware that many of the church's theological and moral principles have their roots in the Jewish scriptures, and that many Christian liturgies and prayers owe much to patterns of worship that can be traced back to the Jewish Bible and to the practices of the Jewish worshipping community. The Vatican II 'Declaration on the Relationship of the Church to Non-Christian Religions', or, to give it is official title, *Nostra Aetate* (promulgated in 1965), refers to facts like these when it 'recalls the spiritual bond linking the people of the New Covenant with Abraham's stock' (*Nostra Aetate*, no 4). Other Christian churches have made similar statements about the relationship between Jews and Christians. The Lutheran Church of Bavaria, for example, in its document 'Christians and Jews' (published in 1998) made the following statement:

> Because Jesus of Nazareth belonged to the Jewish people and was rooted in its religious traditions Christians are brought into a unique relationship with Jews and their faith, [a relationship] that is distinct from the relationship to other religions.

St Paul expressed similar ideas in strikingly imaginative language when he reminded his non-Jewish readers that they were 'a wild olive shoot' that has been grafted on to 'the rich root of the olive tree', which is Israel (see Rom 11:17-18). In plain language Paul is saying that Gentile Christians are now given a share in the privileges that once belonged to Israel alone. In another short passage in the same letter (9:4-5) Paul lists some of these privileges. The Israelites, he said, are the adopted children of God; they experienced the glorious presence of God during their journey through the wilderness and on Mount Sinai (see Exod 16:10; 24:16-17); they were the beneficiaries of the covenants that had been made with the Patriarchs and with Moses (see Gen 15:18; Exod 24:7-8); they regarded the Law that was given on Sinai as a special sign of God's love for them; the splendid cult of the Jerusalem Temple was their pride and joy; the promises made, for example, to Abraham (Gen 12:2) and David (2 Sam 7:11-16) assured them of a great future; their greatest boast was that the Messiah would come from their race.

Polemics and Persecution

So Paul, writing in the days of the church's infancy, and church documents like *Nostra Aetate* that have been formulated in the last half century, acknowledge and celebrate the privileges and the glory of Israel. However, during the nineteen hundred years between Paul and Vatican II the relationships between Jews and Christians were marked by enmity, suspicion and polemics, and by Christian humiliation and persecution of Jews. This is the dark side of Christian history, a catalogue of dismal deeds done by our predecessors in the faith in the name of truth as they saw it.

Even in the New Testament we find texts that can give rise to anti-Jewish feeling. For example, the words 'Crucify him' (Mk 15:13-14; see also Mt 27:25; 1 Thess 2:14-16) have been used to justify the accusation that the Jews are deicides, killers of the Christ. In the early second century Christian writers were asserting that the Jews could no longer claim to be God's people because they had refused to acknowledge Jesus as the Messiah and had crucified him. As Christians saw it, the church was now the new Israel of God and the heir to God's covenant promises. They claimed that the Jewish scriptures were of value only as a preparation for Christ and for the gospel, and that the Jews failed to understand the true meaning of their own Bible.

Many of the Fathers of the church (e.g. Jerome, Ambrose, John Chrysostom) spoke and wrote in bitterly hostile and negative terms against the Jews. From the end of the fourth century, when Christianity became the state religion, the Jews gradually became the victims of discrimination on political and religious grounds. Nevertheless, the Jews remained faithful to their ancestral religion, and managed to survive as a despised minority during the centuries that followed. Indeed, many Jews were eminently successful as traders and in the financial world of the day.

From the thirteenth century onwards, life became even more difficult for the Jewish minority in Europe. The Fourth Lateran Council (1215) obliged Jews to wear a distinctive type of clothing, deprived them of the right to take public office, imposed certain taxes on them, and subjected them to other restrictions, so that Jews were reduced to a pariah status in European society. In 1242 twenty-four wagon loads of Jewish books, totalling thousands of volumes, were burned in Paris, and throughout the rest of the thirteenth century burnings of the Talmud took place in many places throughout Europe. In 1290 all Jews were banished from England and had their properties confiscated, and the same was to happen in several European countries in later centuries. In Spain in the late fifteenth century thousands of Jews fell victim to the Inquisition, and in 1492 all Jews were expelled from that country.

During all these centuries, many church representatives preached against the Jews, portraying them as murderers of Christ, condemning their religion as a religion of law and fear, and ridiculing their ritual observances. The church's attitude to the Jews was summed up in the term 'perfidious Jews', a phrase that had a place in the Good Friday liturgy in the Roman Missal until it was removed by Pope John XXIII. The ultimate disaster overtook the Jews in the twentieth century in Christian Europe when, during the Holocaust, six million Jews were put to death simply because they were Jews. This time, however, the motivation for this ruthless genocide was not religious but racist, although it must be admitted that the religious anti-Judaism of the churches, and of the Christian people in general, facilitated the rise of the murderous anti-Semitism of the Hitler regime.

The Ghetto

The ghetto was a section of a city or town that was designated as an area in which the Jews of that city or town were obliged to live. It was usually surrounded by a wall in which there were one or more gates. The gates remained closed at night. The word 'ghetto' most probably derives from the area in Venice which in 1516 was designated as the only area in that city in which Jews could settle. This area was near a foundry – 'getto' or 'ghetto' in the dialect of Venice. Another possibility is that the word derives from the Italian 'borghetto', a small section of a town. Whatever may be said about the origin of the word 'ghetto', Jews in Europe had spontaneously chosen to live in 'Jewish quarters' since the tenth century. It was only in the sixteenth century that they were obliged to live in a particular part of a town, in a ghetto, where they formed a self-governing community within the wider society. In spite of the severe restrictions imposed on them by the ghetto, the Jews felt secure there. Life within the ghetto was regulated by Jewish law (e.g. marriage laws, Sabbath laws), and lawsuits were judged by Jewish courts. Within the ghetto the Jews maintained their own dignity, followed their own system of education, and observed their own dietary laws. Provided the Jews paid their taxes the civil rulers allowed the situation to continue.

The Jewish Response

Since European Jews lived in lands where a triumphant church had the support of the political powers, there was little they could do in response to the injustices they had to endure. They had to be very circumspect in what they said in public or wrote about the church and Christianity. They did, however, develop their own communal life, and their rabbis promoted a system of prayer, the celebration of the Sabbath and the Jewish festivals, and study of the Jewish sacred texts. All of this confirmed the people in their faith, and strengthened their sense of belonging to the chosen people. We do not find explicit anti-Christian polemics in the Talmud, but this is not surprising, since the Jewish texts were subject to Christian censorship.

From about the seventh century onwards anti-Christian writings began to appear. One expression of the Jewish polemic was the 'Life of Jesus', known in Hebrew as *Toledot Yeshu*, which dates from about the tenth century but which is based on older sources. It is in fact an anthology of Talmudic texts to denigrate Jesus and Christianity. The 'Life' presents Jesus as an illegitimate son of Mary by a Roman soldier, and as a magician who strayed from the teaching of his ancestors.

In the thirteenth and fourteenth centuries Jews were forced to engage in 'Disputations' with spokesmen for the church. These 'disputations' were arranged by the church authorities, and were intended to prove that the Jewish religion was obsolete and that Christianity was the only valid faith. Fortunately the artificial 'disputations' of the past have now given way to authentic dialogue between Jewish and Christian spokespersons who seek to understand the other's faith and who are interested in promoting a harmonious co-existence of the members of the two religions.

A New Beginning

All Christians now recognise the injustice and the cruelty of the ways in which the followers of Christ have treated the Jews for almost two millennia. The unspeakable horror of the Holocaust shocked many thinking Christians, and convinced them that a new era in Jewish-Christian relations had to be inaugurated. The Roman Catholic sense of guilt about the dark centuries when it persecuted and humiliated the Jews is expressed in a prayer for forgiveness which the Pope said during a solemn ceremony of repentance in St Peter's Basilica on 12 March 2000. The Pope's prayer reads as follows:

God of our fathers,
you chose Abraham and his descendants
to bring your name to the nations:
we are deeply saddened by the behaviour of those
who in the course of history
have caused these children of yours to suffer,
and asking your forgiveness
we wish to commit ourselves
to genuine brotherhood with the people of the covenant.

Jewish leaders for their part have responded positively to the new approach which Christians have taken to Judaism. The tenor of the response of some Jews at least may be gauged from 'A Jewish Statement on Christians and Christianity' which was published in September 2000 under the Hebrew title *Dabru Emeth*, which means 'Speak the Truth'. In the course of this short document readers are reminded that Jews and Christians share many truths and moral principles that are taught in the Bible. These shared beliefs, the authors claim, can be the basis for a powerful witness to all humanity, and they can motivate shared activities for improving the lives of our fellow human beings, and for standing against the immoralities and idolatries that harm and degrade us. Such witness, the authors assert, is especially needed after the unprecedented horrors of the past century. The debates that followed the publication of *Dabru Emeth* show that there are many Jews who do not share the optimism of its authors. Indeed, they vehemently reject some of the views of those authors. But at least, the dialogue has begun, and it is to be hoped that as it proceeds, Jews and Christians will come closer to each other and will grow in mutual respect.

CHAPTER FOURTEEN

The Holocaust

The horrors of the Hitler genocide are sharply etched in the memory of both Jews and Christians. For the Jews who can recite a very long litany of persecutions and pogroms, and for the people of Europe that can chronicle an almost endless series of cruel wars and pitiless slaughters, this was the most fiendish manifestation of 'man's inhumanity to man' that had ever been devised. This was not the work of some fanatical leader, or the violent attack of an unrestrained mob, but a plan that had been conceived by the leaders of the Nazi party, and implemented by the highly efficient human and technological resources of a powerful state.

When referring to that hellish tragedy that befell the Jewish people, Jews who write in English tend to avoid the word Holocaust which has a religious connotation. Instead they use the Hebrew word 'Shoah', 'annihilation, catastrophe'. The English word 'holocaust' comes to us from the Latin Bible. We find it, for example, in Gen 22:2; Lev 1:3; Ps 51:16 (NRSV: 'burnt offering'). The Hebrew 'shoah' occurs, for example, in the Hebrew Bible in Is 47:11 (NRSV 'ruin').

When Hitler came to power in 1933 he soon began to enact anti-Jewish legislation. The Nuremberg laws of 1935 deprived Jews of German citizenship. Anyone with even one Jewish grandparent was considered Jewish. Jews were considered to be 'non-Aryan', a foreign race. They were barred from almost all professions. Violence against the Jews and the boycott of Jewish businesses became common. Jews were often forced to sell their commercial properties. Jewish books were burned. On the night of the 9-10 November 1938 synagogues were burned down and

Jewish businesses looted throughout Germany. This night became known in German as 'Kristallnacht', 'The Night of the Broken Glass', and it is now commemorated annually in many Jewish communities.

As the Nazis gained control of other countries, the anti-Jewish campaign spread to Austria, Poland, the Netherlands, Belgium, France etc. In 1941, at Wansee in Berlin, the decision to exterminate all Jews was taken. This decision became known as 'The Final Solution'. For the purpose of carrying out the proposed genocide 'death camps', or 'concentration camps', were erected, mainly in Poland. At the largest of these, Auschwitz, about a million Jews lost their lives. In all, about 6,000,000 Jews, men, women and children, were murdered during the horrors of the Hitler regime.

Today it is almost impossible to understand how such a highly civilised nation as Germany could perpetrate such a barbarous atrocity. And it is shameful to recall that the rest of the world failed to make any meaningful protest against Hitler's treatment of the Jews, and that countries that could have opened their borders to Jews who wanted to escape from Nazi Germany, refused to do so. A document published by the Vatican in 1998 refers to the Shaoh as 'an unspeakable tragedy which can never be forgotten', and it makes the point that by their failure to denounce the Nazi atrocities, Christians often shared in the responsibility for the tragedy. On the occasion of the publication of that document, Pope John Paul II said that 'the Shoah remains an indelible stain on the century that is coming to a close'.

One of the consequences of the Holocaust was the almost total destruction of one important branch of Jewish culture, that of the Ashkenazi Jews of Central and Eastern Europe. For more than a thousand years the synagogues, the elementary schools, and the *yeshivoth* of the Rhineland, Poland, Hungary, Czechoslovakia, the Ukraine, Lithuania etc were centres of Jewish education, spirituality, Talmudic scholarship and mysticism. Over the centuries scholars from these areas produced a vast body of religious literature, as well as a huge volume of secular writing in Hebrew, Yiddish and local languages. These thriving centres of learning were decimated by the Nazi atrocities. Much of the literature that was produced there survives, but the cultural world that produced that literature is gone forever.

The Holocaust has left theologians, both Jewish and Christian, with many problems and questions. Jews can ask: Where was God during the Holocaust? How could a God whom we call our Redeemer, and whom we proclaim to be all-powerful and infinitely good, allow this to happen to his chosen people? When thousands of pious old Jews, who had manifested lifelong allegiance to their God, cried to him from the gas chambers, why did he not answer their prayers? Why did he allow thousands of innocent children to endure the horrors of the death factories in the camps? Some Jews answer that it makes no sense to speak of God after Auschwitz. God, they say, is dead. But, they add, a resurrection has taken place. Israel has risen from the crematoriums and the mass graves, and lives in the State of Israel. Among the Orthodox there were those who claimed that the Holocaust was a divine punishment for the irreligious ways of those who had abandoned the traditional ways of living the Jewish religion. Other Jews wrestle with the problem of the God who did not intervene, but who is still God. They cannot explain the evil that was the Holocaust, but they have not abandoned their faith in a God who is good. They may not understand God's ways, but they do not reject the God of the ancestors.

Christian theologians for their part know that theology can never be the same after Auschwitz. Did not Christian anti-Judaism feed into Nazi anti-Semitism? Did not terms like 'perfidious Jews', 'obdurate' Jews who refused to accept Jesus as the Messiah, and 'deicides', create an anti-Jewish prejudice among the Christian people? Did not the very term 'New Testament', as commonly understood, devalue the 'Old Testament'? Does not the well-planned murder of 6,000,000 Jews by a people who were mainly Christian call the credibility of the Christian gospel of love and justice into question? As they contemplate the unspeakable horrors of the Shoah, Christians are learning to reject

earlier Christian portrayals of Judaism, and to show greater respect for the Jews and for their religion. They are becoming
aware that they must formulate their theology in a manner that
does not suggest or imply that the Jews have lost their status as
the people of the covenant. At the same time they must remain
true to their convictions concerning the redemptive mission of
Jesus Christ whose grace is available to all, and they must continue their mission to proclaim the good news of Christ to all
peoples.

In the post-Holocaust era the question of God and the question of how we can speak about God have continued to exercise
the minds of both Jewish and Christian thinkers, and in the post-
Nostra Aetate era scholars from both sides have joined forces in
the search for answers to these questions. Pondering on the sacred
traditions of both faiths in a spirit of respectful dialogue, they
hope to learn from each other, to enrich each other, and to overcome the misunderstandings and animosities that have divided
the two communities in the past.

In 1951, the government of Israel established the twenty-sev-
enth day of Nisan, a week after the seventh day of the Feast of
Passover-Unleavened Bread, as a day to commemorate the
Holocaust and its victims. The day is known to Jews by its
Hebrew name, *Yom ha-Shoah*, 'the day [of remembrance] of the
Shoah'. It is observed as a national holiday in Israel, and various
Jewish communities throughout the world organise commemoration services on that day. In most synagogues special services
are held, and in many of them six candles are lit in memory of
the six million Jews who died in the Holocaust. But is not only
Jews who mark Holocaust day. In many countries different civic
and religious groups organise commemoration functions and
services on this day.

No One Spoke Out

Pastor Martin Niemoeller was a Protestant Pastor who openly opposed the Nazis and preached against the Hitler regime until he was
arrested in July 1937. He was eventually condemned, and he spent
the following years until 1945 in concentration camps. After the War
he took a leading part in structuring the 'Stuttgart Confession of
Guilt', which was published in October 1945, and which formally
admitted the guilt of the German Protestant churches for their failure to resist Nazism. Niemoeller's poem, which we will go on to
quote, can be read as an answer to the question: How could the
Holocaust have happened? We cannot be sure of the exact wording
of the original, and we do not know the circumstances in which the
text was composed. But some scholars believe that the following
version brings us close to Niemoeller's own words:

> First they came for the communists, and I did not speak out
> because I was not a communist;
> Then they came for the socialists, and I did not speak out
> because I was not a socialist;
> Then they came for the trade unionists, and I did not speak out
> because I was not a trade unionist;
> Then they came for the Jews, and I did not speak out
> because I was not a Jew;
> Then they came for me;
> and there was no one left to speak out for me.

CHAPTER FIFTEEN

The Jews in Ireland

The earliest reference to the coming of Jews to Ireland is found in the Annals of Inishfallen for 1079: 'Five Jews came over sea with gifts to Tairdelbach and they were sent back again over sea.' The Tairdelbach mentioned was Turlough O'Brien (1009-1086) who was King of Munster and grandson of Brian Boru. The five Jews who are said to have come to our shores may have been merchants who had come from France. It is probable that other Jewish traders came to the country during the following centuries and that some of them settled in Ireland. It is possible that some victims of the expulsion of the Jews from Spain (1492) and Portugal (1496) may have fled to Ireland. But if so, they do not seem to have settled permanently in the country.

A number of Sephardi Jews (i.e. Jews whose ancestors came from Spain and Portugal) may have lived in Dublin during the sixteenth and seventeenth centuries. These would seem to have been mostly of the wealthy merchant class. In about the year 1660 there was a Jewish prayer room in Crane Lane, opposite Dublin Castle. Towards the end of the seventeenth century, as a result of the wars in Europe, many poor Jews fled from Germany and Poland to England. Some of these Ashkenazi Jews (i.e. Jews from Germany and Eastern Europe) travelled on to Ireland where they became engaged in peddling and in petty trade. They worshipped with their Sephardi co-religionists in the synagogue in Crane Lane. In 1718 the Jewish community leased a plot as a cemetery at Ballybough near Fairview, in Dublin. It is estimated that in 1745 there were about 200 Jews living in Ireland. In the 1760s the synagogue was moved from Crane Lane to Marlborough Green, near the site of the present Custom House.

From the 1780s the Jewish population of Dublin declined due to the political unrest that was common in the Ireland of that time, to trade depression, intermarriage, conversion etc. Many Jews left for England or for America. In 1790, for lack of worshippers, the Marlborough synagogue closed down.

An Expanding Community

After the Napoleonic Wars, from about 1820 onwards, a number of Ashkenazi Jews, mainly from Germany, Poland and Holland arrived in Ireland. Having worshipped for some years in a private house, the congregation acquired a premises in 12 Mary's Abbey, off Capel St in 1836. According to the 1861 census, there were 393 Jews in Ireland in that year. Up to 1880 the number of Jews in the country never exceeded 350.

The Jews who arrived in Ireland in the early part of the nineteenth century had one thing in common with the Catholic population. Both communities were deprived of certain civil rights, and they were excluded from certain areas of public life. Daniel O'Connell, who struggled to gain Catholic Emancipation, supported a Bill for the Emancipation of the Jews which passed the House of Commons, but which was rejected by the Lords in 1831. Writing to a Jewish leader in England at this time O'Connell said: '… (Ireland) is the only Christian country that I know of unsullied by any one act of persecution against the Jews'. The Jews of Dublin, and especially wealthy Jews in England and in America, gave generous support to the Irish people during the Famine of 1854-57.

Between 1881 and 1901 there was a huge increase in the number of Jews in Dublin. Following the pogroms in Russia in 1881 and in the succeeding years, and frustrated by laws that discriminated against the Jews, many Jews fled the Russian territories. Some of these refugees came to the West and a number of them, mainly Lithuanians, settled in Ireland. It is estimated that between 1881 and 1910 some 2,000 Jews came to this country. Some of the newcomers joined the established communities in Dublin, while others made their homes in Belfast, Cork,

Limerick, Waterford, Derry and Dundalk. Many of them made a living as drapers, hawkers, tailors and general dealers. By 1901 there were over 2,000 Jews in Dublin, over 700 in Belfast, 359 in Cork, and 171 in Limerick. The Jewish population of the whole of Ireland numbered 3,898.

The newly arrived Jews who settled in Dublin lived mainly in the Portobello district of the South Circular Road. The area became known to the locals as 'Little Jerusalem'. In 1892, in response to this population shift, and to accommodate the increased Jewish community, the synagogue in Mary's Abbey was closed and a bigger one opened in Adelaide Road, quite near to the South Circular Road. Rabbi S. Herman Adler, Chief Rabbi of the British Empire, consecrated the new synagogue. On that occasion he said: 'It is said that Ireland is the only country in the world which cannot be charged with persecuting the Jews.' After the 1940s many Jews moved to the suburbs of Terenure and Rathfarnham. In 1946 the Jewish population of the whole of Ireland was 5,381. Of these 3,907 lived in the Republic, and 1,474 in Northern Ireland. These 1946 figures represent the highest number of Jews ever recorded in the country.

Anti-Semitism in Ireland?

Many of the Jews who settled in Dublin in the early 1880s became pedlars and traders. Some shopkeepers saw them as a threat to their business, and in 1886 placards urging the citizens to have no dealings with the newcomers were posted all over Dublin, and anti-Jewish letters appeared in newspapers. However, the newspapers condemned the movement, and the anti-Jewish protest soon came to an end. On Easter Sunday 1884 a crowd attacked the home of a Jew in Limerick. Stones were thrown through the window and the wife and child of the owner of the house were hurt. The police intervened and two of the ringleaders of the attack were sentenced to a month's imprisonment with hard labour. In 1894 there was a minor anti-Jewish disturbance in Cork. But again, the ringleaders were imprisoned.

By far the most notorious expression of anti-Jewish feeling

occurred in Limerick, a city which had 130 Jewish inhabitants in 1896. Early in 1904 Fr John Creagh, a Redemptorist, preached two sermons to the members of the Archconfraternity of the Holy Family in which he vehemently attacked the Jews of the city, condemning especially the way in which they went as pedlars from door to door persuading people to buy goods at exorbitant prices. He urged his hearers to have no commercial dealings with Jews. The result was that the Jews became the victims of a boy-cott which lasted for two years. Many of them were pauperised, and about eighty members of the community left the city and settled in Cork or emigrated. The number of Jews who remained in Limerick may have been less than forty. During the conflict Michael Davitt, founder of the Land League, and John Redmond, leader of the Home Rule Party, spoke out in defence of the Jews. On the other hand, Arthur Griffith's paper, *The United Irishman*, was on the side of Fr Creagh. In 1906, Fr Creagh, having finished one term as director of the Archconfraternity, departed for the Redemptorists' new missions in the Philippines.

In the 1940s there was another manifestation of anti-Judaism, when the members of Maria Duce, a movement that was founded by Fr Denis Fahey in 1945. Fr Fahey was convinced that the Jews were in league with Freemasons and communists, and that to-gether they planned a world conspiracy. He claimed that the Jews were behind Bolshevism in Russia, and that the Jews and the Freemasons controlled the United States, the United Nations and international business. He also called into question the loy-alty of Irish Jews to the Irish State. Father Fahey's movement, which never had a great following, declined steadily in the 1950s and petered out in the 1960s.

The Recent Past

During the Second World War, when European Jews were being rounded up and sent to the Nazi death camps, the Irish govern-ment was less than generous in opening the country's doors to Jewish refugees. The then Taoiseach, Éamon de Valera, who, over the years had a good relationship with the Dublin Jewish community leaders, and especially with Dr Isaac Herzog, the Chief Rabbi, tried to respond to requests to save individual Jews who were in danger of being sent to the gas chambers. But he did not authorise the kind of distribution of Irish passports that would have helped many Jews to escape. The number of Jews allowed into Ireland during the war years may have been as few as sixty. In 1995, on the occasion of an official ceremony to mark the fiftieth anniversary of the liberation of Bergen-Belsen and to honour the memory of the six million European Jews who died in the Holocaust, the Fine Gael TD Alan Shatter, who is Jewish, stated that there never had been an official expression of regret from any Irish government at the state's refusal to admit into Ireland many Jews who were fleeing from Nazi terror. In spite of de Valera's failure to manifest the magnanimity that the Jews might have expected of him during the Nazi period, the Jewish community continued to hold him in high esteem. In 1963, when he was President, the Irish Jewish community decided to honour him by planting a forest of 10,000 trees in Israel as a mark of recognition of his work for peace and freedom, especially the freedom of small nations. On that occasion tributes were paid to de Valera as a stalwart well-wisher of Jewry and of the Jewish State. However, many Jews throughout the world, and many others as well, who know nothing about de Valera's friendship with and support of the Jews, or about the Jewish tributes that were paid to him, will know about his visit to the German Embassy in May 1945 to express his condolences on the death of Hitler. That visit shocked many people, especially Jews, in many parts of the world at the time, and it has continued to puzzle people ever since.

In modern Ireland, Jews have made significant contributions to the cultural, professional and political life of the country. The large number of Jews who have been involved in the medical and legal professions is out of all proportion to the number of Jews in the country. The first Jew to make an impact on the political scene was Robert Briscoe, who was elected as a TD in 1927, and who continued to serve in Dáil Éireann until 1965. He was elected Lord Mayor of Dublin in 1956, and he held that position for a second time in 1961-62. His son, Ben, succeeded him in Dáil Éireann in 1965, and he too became Lord Mayor of Dublin, having been elected in 1988. In the 1992 general election three Jews were elected to the Dáil. These were Ben Briscoe (Fianna Fáil), Mervyn Taylor (Labour) and Alan Shatter (Fine Gael).

The 2002 national census revealed that for the first time since 1946 there was a small increase in the Jewish population of the Irish Republic. According to that census there were 1790 Jews in the Republic, of whom 1200 lived in Dublin. Among the many foreign-born people who have come to Ireland in recent years there have been a number of Jews who have taken up permanent residence here, or who are on short-to-medium contracts with different companies. Nevertheless, the fact remains that many young Jewish people, often with a view to meeting a Jewish spouse, move to Israel or to cities in England and America that have large Jewish communities. It is clear that such departures, if continued, must inevitably lead to a decline in the growth rate of the already small number of Irish Jews.

CHAPTER SIXTEEN

Official Church Documents Relating to the Jews

LUMEN GENTIUM

It is difficult to overstate the dramatic changes that have taken place in Christian attitudes to the Jews since the Holocaust. The following extracts from Roman documents show how the Roman Catholic Church in the course of the last half-century struggled with the tasks of establishing a new relationship with the Jews, of formulating a new understanding of Judaism, and of bringing about a change of attitude to Jews and Judaism among Catholics. Similar documents have been issued by nearly all the mainline Christian denominations.

The Dogmatic Constitution on the Church (*Lumen Gentium*), which was approved by the Fathers of the Second Vatican Council on 21 November 1964, contains a short passage which focuses on the privileged status of the Jewish people, the chosen people of God. In this very short passage, the Church, for the first time in almost 2,000 years, took a positive view of Judaism and proclaimed the glories of the Jewish people. The section dealing with the Jews, which occurs in paragraph 16 of that important document, reads as follows:

> ... those who have not yet accepted the gospel are related to the People of God [that is, to the Church] in various ways. There is, first, that people to which the covenants and promises were made, and from whom Christ was born in the flesh (cf Rom 9:4-5); in view of the divine choice, they are a people most dear for the sake of the fathers, for the gifts of God are without repentance (cf Rom 11:28-29).
>
> (See A. Flannery (ed), *Vatican Council II. The Conciliar and Post Conciliar Documents* (Dublin: Dominican Publications, 1981), 367.)

NOSTRA AETATE

On 28 October 1965, the Vatican II Declaration on the Relation of
the Church to Non-Christian Religions, or *Nostra Aetate*, was
published. Paragraph 4 of this document dealt with the church's
relation to the Jews and Judaism, and it was destined to become
an important landmark in the history of the relationship between Jews and Christians. It put an official end to centuries of
bitterness and hostility between the Roman Catholic Church
and the Jews, and it opened the way to an era where the two
faith communities can maintain their distinctiveness while re-
specting each other and working together for the betterment of
human society. What follows is the full text of *Nostra Aetate*, par 4.

Sounding the depths of the mystery which is the church, this
sacred council remembers the spiritual ties which link the
people of the New Covenant to the stock of Abraham.

The church of Christ acknowledges that in God's plan of
salvation the beginning of her faith and election is to be
found in the patriarchs, Moses and the prophets. She professes
that all Christ's faithful, who as people of faith are children of
Abraham (cf Gal 3:7), are included in the same patriarch's
call and that the salvation of the church is mystically prefig-
ured in the exodus of God's chosen people from the land of
bondage. On this account the church cannot forget that she
received the revelation of the Old Testament by way of that
people with whom God in his inexpressible mercy established the ancient covenant. Nor can she forget that she
draws nourishment from that good olive tree onto which the
wild olive branches of the Gentiles have been grafted (cf Rom
11:17-24). The church believes that Christ who is our peace
has through his cross reconciled Jews and Gentiles and made
them one in himself (cf Eph 2:14-16).

Likewise, the church keeps ever before her mind the
words of the apostle Paul about his kinsmen: 'They are
Israelites, and to them belong the sonship, the glory, the
covenants, the giving of the law, the worship and the promises;
to them belong the patriarchs, and of their race according to

the flesh, is the Christ (cf Rom 9:4-5), the son of the virgin Mary. She is mindful, moreover, that the apostles, the pillars on which the church stands, are of Jewish descent, as are many of those early disciples who proclaimed the gospel of Christ to the world.

As holy scripture testifies, Jerusalem did not recognise God's moment when it came (cf Lk 19:42). Jews for the most part did not accept the gospel; on the contrary, many opposed the spreading of it (cf Rom 11:28). Even so, the apostle Paul maintains that the Jews remain very dear to God, for the sake of the patriarchs, since God does not take back the gifts he bestowed or the choice he made (cf Rom 11:28-29; also *Lumen Gentium* 16). Together with the prophets and that same apostle, the church awaits the day, known to God alone, when all peoples will call on God with one voice and 'serve him shoulder to shoulder' (Zeph 3:9; cf Is 66:23; Ps 65:4; Rom 11:11-32).

Since Christians and Jews have such a common spiritual heritage, this sacred council wishes to encourage and further mutual understanding and appreciation. This can be obtained, especially, by way of biblical and theological enquiry and through friendly discussions.

Even though the Jewish authorities and those who followed their lead pressed for the death of Christ (cf Jn 19:6), neither all Jews indiscriminately at that time, nor Jews today, can be charged with the crimes committed during his passion. It is true that the church is the new people of God, yet the Jews should not be spoken of as rejected or accursed as if this followed from holy scripture. Consequently, all must take care, lest in catechising or in preaching the Word of God, they teach anything which is not in accord with the truth of the gospel message or the spirit of Christ.

Indeed, the church reproves every form of persecution against whomsoever it may be directed. Remembering, then, her common heritage with the Jews, and moved not by any political consideration, but solely by the religious motivation of Christian charity, she deplores all hatreds, persecutions, displays of anti-Semitism levelled at any time or from any source against the Jews.

The church always held and continues to hold that Christ out of infinite love underwent suffering and death because of the sins of all men, so that all might attain salvation. It is the duty of the church, therefore, in her preaching to proclaim the cross of Christ as the sign of God's universal love and the source of all grace.

(See Flannery (ed), *Vatican Council II*, pp 740-742.)

GUIDLINES ON RELIGIOUS RELATIONS WITH THE JEWS
1 December 1974

On 22 October, 1974, Pope Paul VI established the Commission for Religious Relations with the Jews. Within two weeks, on 1 December, the Commission published the 'Guidelines'. The purpose of this document, as stated in its Introduction, was to 'propose some first practical applications in different essential areas of the church's life, with a view to launching or developing sound relations between Catholics and their Jewish brothers and sisters.' Having referred to some of the main themes of *Nostra Aetate*, the authors of the 'Guidelines,' from which we now give some extracts, discussed the following topics:

I. Dialogue
... Dialogue presupposes that each side wishes to know the other, and wishes to increase and deepen its knowledge of the other. It constitutes a particularly suitable means of favouring a better mutual knowledge and, especially in the case of dialogue between Jews and Christians, of probing the riches of one's own tradition. Dialogue demands respect for the other as he or she is; above all, respect for the other's faith and his or her religious convictions. ... In addition to friendly talks, competent people will be encouraged to meet and to study together the many problems deriving from the fundamental convictions of Judaism and of Christianity. ...

II. Liturgy

The existing links between the Christian liturgy and the Jewish liturgy will be borne in mind. ... To improve Jewish-Christian relations, it is important to take cognisance of those common elements of the liturgical life (formulas, feasts, rites, etc.) in which the Bible holds an essential place. ... An effort will be made to acquire a better understanding of whatever in the Old Testament retains its own perpetual value (cf *Dei Verbum*, n 14-15), since that has not been cancelled by the later interpretations of the New Testament. Rather, the New Testament brings out the full meaning of the Old, while both Old and New illumine and explain each other (cf *ibid.*, n 16). ... When commenting on biblical texts, emphasis will be laid on the continuity of our faith with that of the earlier Covenant, in the perspective of the promises, without minimising those elements of Christianity which are original. ... With respect to liturgical readings, care will be taken to see that homilies based on them will not distort their meaning, especially when it is a question of passages which seem to show the Jewish people as such in an unfavourable light. ...

III. Teaching and Education

... Judaism in the time of Christ and the apostles was a complex reality, embracing many different trends, many spiritual, religious, social and cultural values. ...

The Old Testament and the Jewish tradition founded upon it must not be set against the New Testament in such a way that the former seems to constitute a religion of only justice, fear and legalism, with no appeal to the love of God and neighbour (cf Deut 6:5; Lev 19:18; Mt 22:34-40). ...

Jesus was born of the Jewish people, as were his apostles and a large number of his first disciples. ... although his teaching had a profoundly new character, Christ nevertheless, in many instances, took his stand on the teaching of the Old Testament. ...

With regard to the trial and death of Jesus, the council recalled that 'what happened in his passion cannot be blamed upon all the Jews then living, without distinction, nor upon the Jews of today' (*Nostra Aetate*, n 4). ...

The history of Judaism did not end with the destruction of Jerusalem, but rather went on to develop a religious tradition.

... Information concerning these questions is important at all levels of Christian instruction and education. Among sources of information, special attention should be paid to the following:

catechisms and religious textbooks

history books

the mass-media (press, radio, cinema, television). ...

The effective use of these means presupposes the thorough formation of instructors and educators in training schools, seminaries and universities.

IV. Joint Social Action

... Jewish and Christian tradition, founded on the Word of God, is aware of the value of the human person, the image of God. Love of the same God must show itself in effective action for the good of humankind. In the spirit of the prophets, Jews and Christians will work together, seeking social justice and peace at every level – local, national and international. ... At the same time, such collaboration can do much to foster mutual understanding and esteem.

(See Flannery (ed), *Vatican Council II*, pp 743-749.)

MAINZ 1980: THE COVENANT NEVER REVOKED

The sermon which Pope John Paul II made in Mainz on 17 November 1980 is frequently quoted, because in that sermon the Pope stated explicitly that God's covenant with the people of Israel has never been revoked. This statement brought to an end the centuries old Christian claim that the Jews had been rejected by God and had ceased to be his chosen people.

... The concrete brotherly relations between Jews and Catholics in Germany assume a quite particular value against the grim background of the persecution and the at-

tempted extermination of Judaism in this country. The innocent victims in Germany and elsewhere, the families destroyed or dispersed, the cultural values or art treasures destroyed forever, are a tragic proof of where discrimination
and contempt of human dignity can lead .... The depth and
richness of our common heritage are revealed to us particularly in friendly dialogue and trusting collaboration. I rejoice
that, in this country, conscience and zealous care is dedicated
to all this. Many public and private initiatives in the pastoral,
academic, and social field serve this purpose ... The first dimension of this dialogue, that is, the meeting between the
people of God of the Old Covenant, never revoked by God
(cf Rom 11:29), and that of the New Covenant, is at the same
time a dialogue within our church, that is to say, between the
first and the second part of her Bible ... A second dimension
of our dialogue — the true and central one — is the meeting
between present-day Christian churches and the present-day
people of the Covenant concluded with Moses. ... I would
also like to refer briefly to a third dimension of our dialogue.
The German bishops dedicated the concluding chapter of
their declaration to the tasks which we have in common.
Jews and Christians, as children of Abraham, are called to be
a blessing for the world (cf Gen 12:2ff.), by committing themselves together for peace and justice among all men and peoples ...

> (The full text of the Pope's speech in Mainz may be found
> in E. J. Fisher and L. Klenicki (eds), *Spiritual Pilgrimage.*
> *Pope John Paul II. Texts on Jews and Judaism 1979-1995* (New
> York: Crossroad, 1995), pp 13-16.)

THE ROMAN SYNAGOGUE

The Pope's visit to Rome's central Synagogue on 13 April 1986
was a truly historic event, a symbolic gesture of great significance. Not surprisingly the occasion attracted the attention of
media representatives from around the world. I give here some
of the key passages from the Pope's speech on that occasion.

... This gathering in a way brings to a close, after the pontific-
ate of John XXIII and the Second Vatican Council, a long period
which we must not tire of reflecting upon in order to draw
from it the appropriate lessons. Certainly, we cannot and
should not forget that the historical circumstances of the past
were very different from those that have laboriously mat-
ured over the centuries. The general acceptance of a legitimate plurality on the social, civil, and religious levels has
been arrived at with great difficulty. Nevertheless, a consideration of centuries-long cultural conditioning could not pre-
vent us from recognising that the acts of discrimination, un-
justified limitation of religious freedom, oppression also on
the level of civil freedom in regard to the Jews were, from an
objective point of view, gravely deplorable manifestations.
Yes, once again, through myself, the church, in the words of
the well-known declaration *Nostra Aetate* (no 4), 'deplores the
hatred, persecutions, and displays of anti-Semitism directed
against the Jews at any time and by anyone.' I repeat: 'by
anyone.'

I would like once more to express a word of abhorrence
for the genocide decreed against the Jewish people during
the last war, which led to the Holocaust of millions of innocent victims.

The Jewish community of Rome, too, paid a high price in
blood. ... Today's visit is meant to make a decisive contribution to the consolidation of the good relations between our
two communities, in imitation of the example of so many
men and women who have worked and who are still working today, on both sides, to overcome old prejudices and to
secure ever wider and fuller recognition of that 'bond' and
that 'common spiritual patrimony' that exist between Jews
and Christians.

We are all aware that, among the riches of this paragraph
number four of *Nostra Aetate*, three points are especially relevant. I would like to underline them here, before you today,
in this truly unique circumstance.

The first is that the church of Christ discovers her 'bond' with Judaism by 'searching into her own mystery' (cf *Nostra Aetate*, no 4). The Jewish religion is not 'extrinsic' to us, but in a certain way 'intrinsic' to our religion. With Judaism, therefore, we have a relationship which we do not have with any other religion. You are our dearly beloved brothers and, in a certain way, it could be said that you are our elder brothers.

The second point noted by the council is that no ancestral or collective blame can be imputed to the Jews as a people for 'what happened in Christ's passion' (cf *Nostra Aetate*, no 4) – not indiscriminately to the Jews of that time, nor to those who came afterwards, not to those of today. So any alleged theological justification for discriminatory measures or, worse still, for acts of persecution, is unfounded. ...

The third point I would like to emphasise [is that] ... it is not lawful to say that the Jews are 'repudiated or cursed,' as if this were taught or deduced from the sacred scriptures of the Old or the New Testament (cf *Nostra Aetate*, no 4).

... we wish to deepen dialogue in loyalty and friendship in respect for one another's intimate convictions, taking as a fundamental basis the elements of the revelation which we have in common, as a 'great spiritual patrimony' (cf *Nostra Aetate*, no 4).

(The full text of the Pope's speech in the synagogue of Rome may be found in Fisher and Klenicki (eds), *Spiritual Pilgrimage. Pope John Paul II*, pp 60-66.)

THE ROOTS OF ANTI-SEMITISM

From 31 October to 1 November 1997 sixty international scholars gathered in Rome to take part in a symposium on 'The Roots of Anti-Judaism'. In an address to the participants in that symposium Pope John Paul II, having acknowledged that in the past many church members nurtured feelings of hostility towards the Jews and treated them unjustly, expressed his conviction that the deliberations of the assembled scholars would show that anti-Semitism has no justification and is absolutely reprehensible. Once again, as at Mainz, the Pope declared that the Jewish people are still the people of God. We take the following extracts from that Papal address:

... in the Christian world – I do not say on the part of the Christian church itself – erroneous and unjust interpretations of the New Testament regarding the Jewish people and their alleged culpability [e.g. 1 Thess 2:14-16; Phil 3:2-6; Gal 4:21-31; Mt 27:25; Jn 8:44 ; *added by M.M.*] have circulated for too long, engendering feelings of hostility towards this people. They contributed to the lulling of consciences, so that when the wave of persecutions inspired by a pagan anti-Semitism, which in essence is equivalent to an anti-Christianity, swept across Europe, alongside Christians who did everything to save the persecuted even at the risk of their lives, the spiritual resistance of many was not what humanity rightfully expected from the disciples of Christ. Your lucid examination of the past, in view of a purification of memory, is particularly appropriate for clearly showing that anti-Semitism has no justification and is absolutely reprehensible. ...

The fact of divine election is at the origin of this small people [Israel] situated between the great pagan empires whose brilliant culture overshadowed them. This people was gathered together and led by God, the Creator of heaven and earth. ... This people perseveres in spite of everything because they are the people of the Covenant, and despite human infidelities, the Lord is faithful to his Covenant. ... The scriptures cannot be separated from the people and its history which leads to Christ the promised and awaited Messiah. ... That is why those who regard the fact that Jesus was a Jew and that his milieu was the Jewish world as mere cultural accidents, for which one could substitute another religious tradition from which the Lord's person could be separated without losing his identity, not only ignore the meaning of salvation history, but more radically challenge the very truth of the incarnation and make a genuine concept of inculturation impossible. ...

The church firmly condemns all forms of genocide, as well as the racist theories that have inspired them and have claimed to justify them. ... Racism is thus a negation of the deepest identity of the human being who is a person created in the image and likeness of God.

(The full text of the Pope's address may be found in *L'Osservatore Romano*, Weekly English Edition, 5 November 1997, pp 1-2.)

CONFESSION OF SINS AGAINST THE PEOPLE OF ISRAEL

On the 12 March 2000, Pope John Paul II celebrated a solemn liturgy in St Peter's in Rome, in the course of which he prayed for forgiveness for the sins committed by the sons and daughters of the church during the centuries. There were seven prayers in all, the fourth of which was 'A confession of sins against the people of Israel.' What follows is the text of that prayer:

Let us pray that, in recalling the sufferings endured by the people of Israel throughout history, Christians will acknowledge the sins committed by not a few of their number against the people of the Covenant and the blessings, and in this way will purify their hearts.

God of our fathers, you chose Abraham and his descendants to bring your Name to the nations: we are deeply saddened by the behaviour of those who in the course of history have caused these children of yours to suffer, and asking your forgiveness we wish to commit ourselves to genuine brotherhood with the people of the Covenant. We ask this through Christ our Lord.

(The text of this prayer has been published in *L'Osservatore Romano*, Weekly English Edition, 22 March, 2000, p 4.)

Short Glossary of Jewish Terms

Aggadah: see below 'Haggadah'.

Emancipation: In medieval Europe the Jews were often obliged to live in ghettoes or other designated areas; they were not allowed to own land or to practise certain trades and professions. The emancipation of the Jews, i.e. the removal of these and other limitations, and the granting of full citizenships to Jews, came about in Europe at the end of the eighteenth century as a result of the Enlightenment and the French Revolution. In 1791 the Jews of France received all the rights of French citizenship. Jews in America had been granted full equality by the Constitution that came into effect in 1789. Following Catholic Emancipation in England in 1829, the English Jews began to agitate for a comparable emancipation. They were gradually admitted to different professions, and by 1890 they had gained access to all public and academic positions. In the wake of the 1848 revolution in Germany, Jews of that country achieved legal equality. However, Jews were treated differently in different states within Germany. The Austrian Emperor, Joseph II, issued the Edict of Tolerance in 1782. This granted certain freedoms to the Jews, but it was only in 1867 that the Constitution ended discrimination on the basis of religion.

Fringes: 'fringes' is the name given to the tassels worn by men, in accordance with the prescription of Num 15:37-41, at the four corners of a tallith. The rabbis taught that the 'fringes' serve as a reminder to Jews of their duty to observe the Laws of the Torah (see Num 15:39). The 'fringes' are mentioned in Mt 23:5.

Haggadah, or *Aggadah:* The word 'haggadah' is used to refer to a certain body of Jewish literature that comments on and amplifies the biblical text in a very imaginative fashion. 'The Haggadah' is also the name given to a book that contains the ritual for the Passover Seder.

Halakah, literally 'walking', is the name given to the body of legal prescriptions that regulate the personal, social, and religious behaviour of Jews.

Havdalah is a short ritual that takes place at the end of the Sabbath to mark the distinction between the holy day and the working days.

Kaddish: the Aramaic word *kaddish* means 'sanctification,' and the Aramaic prayer which is known as the 'Kaddish' is a doxology, a prayer of praise. The Kaddish is not recited unless there is a *minyan* present.

Karaites: a Jewish sect that claims to have been founded by the eighth-century Babylonian teacher Anan ben David. The Karaites broke with Rabbinic Judaism, rejected the authority of the Oral Torah, and asserted that the Bible is the only authoritative expression of God's will. The group flourished between the late ninth and the late eleventh centuries CE. Today there are about twenty-five thousand Karaites in Israel, as well as small communities in such places as Istanbul, France and the United States.

Ketubah: a marriage contract. This is a legally binding document that specifies a husband's obligations towards his wife, and that establishes a woman's marriage and divorce rights. Having been carefully drawn up in advance, it is handed to a Jewish bride during the marriage ceremony.

Kiddush: the Hebrew word *kiddush* means 'sanctification', and the ritual that is known by that name is a prayer of blessing that is recited over a cup of wine in the home or in the synagogue to sanctify the Sabbath or a festival.

Kippah: see below 'skullcap'.

Kosher: This word is most commonly used to refer to food that is fit for consumption according to the Jewish dietary laws. But it can also be used to refer to other objects that are in conformity with ritual laws. It can, for example, be said that a *mikveh* is kosher, if it is constructed and serviced according to all the appropriate rabbinic laws.

Mehitzah: a partition which separates men from women in Orthodox synagogues.

Mezuzah: A mezuzah is a little oblong container fixed to the right-hand doorpost of a house. In this container is placed a piece of parchment on which two scripture passages, Deut 6:4-9 and 11:13-21, are written. Each of these passages contains the injunction that the Israelites must write the words of God on the doorposts of their houses and on their gates (see Deut 6:9; 11:20), an injunction which Jews down through the centuries have taken literally. In these two verses the Hebrew word for 'doorpost' is *mezuzah*, and it is this word that gives its name to the ritual object we are considering.

The parchment on which the scripture texts mentioned above are written must be made from the skin of a clean or kosher animal (see the chapter on dietary laws above), and the text of the scripture passages must be written in Hebrew. It is customary to write the text in twenty-two lines, the number of letters in the Hebrew alphabet. Since the text has the status of a Torah text, it cannot be touched, and it is therefore rolled up and placed in a little container made of wood, metal or glass.

We have evidence that the practice of placing the *mezuzah* on doors existed before 100 BCE, and the custom is widely observed by modern Jews. According to Jewish law the *mezuzah* should be fixed to the entrance to every home, and to the door of every room in the house, excluding bathrooms and store rooms. It is customary to place it on the right hand doorpost, in the top third of the door post and slanted, with the upper end pointing inwards. The purpose of the *mezuzah* is to remind the occupants of a house when they go in or go out that the Lord guards the going out and the coming in of those who believe in him (see Ps 121:8). It is the practice of pious people when leaving or entering the house to kiss the *mezuzah*, or to touch it and then kiss their fingers.

Mikveh: In rabbinic literature this term is used to refer to a body of water in which a person immerses himself or herself for the purpose of ritual purification.

Minyan is the term used to designate the quorum of ten male adults, aged thirteen or over, who, according to tradition, must be present before a public liturgical service can take place. Nowadays Reform and Conservative and Reconstructionist communities allow women to be counted as members of a *minyan*.

Mishnah: the *mishnah* is the earliest written collection of Jewish law. It is a core document of the Jewish legal and religious tradition. It was compiled and arranged in six 'orders' by Rabbi Judah, the Prince, in about 200 CE.

Mitzvah (plural *mitzvot*): the basic meaning of this Hebrew word is 'commandment'. There are 613 *mitzvot*, commandments, in the Bible, and very many more have been added by the rabbis. The word *mitzvah* is frequently used with the meaning 'good deed', something that is done because it is pleasing to God, a religious duty, a meritorious action. It is, for example, a *mitzvah* to light the Sabbath candles, to put a *mezuzah* on one's door, to visit the sick, etc.

Nostra Aetate is the Latin title of the document known as the 'Declaration on the Relation of the Church to Non-Christian Religions', that was issued by the Fathers of the Second Vatican Council.

Phylacteries: see below 'Tefillin'.

Prayerbook: see below 'Siddur'.

Prayer Shawl, usually referred to by its Hebrew name '*Tallith*' by Jews. The original meaning of the Hebrew word 'tallith' was 'cloak'. It was a rectangular garment, like a blanket, that was worn by men in ancient times. Num 15:37-41 stipulated that the Israelites should wear 'tassels' on the corners of such garments to remind them of the Law of God and of the commandments they were to obey. So originally the tallith was not associated with prayer. Furthermore, it was not the tallith itself that had a religious significance, but the 'tassels'.

When the tallith ceased to be an ordinary article of clothing,

Jews wore it at prayer in order to continue observing the law of wearing 'tassels'. Because of this it is called a 'prayer shawl'. Some pious Jews wear a tallith all day under their outer garments. The tallith is usually white, and is normally made of wool, though cotton or silk are allowed. In remembrance of the 'cord of blue' referred to in Num 15:38, black (or blue) stripes are usually woven into the tallith.

All Jewish males over thirteen years of age are obliged to wear the tallith, although in some Orthodox synagogues it is worn only by married men. Some Jews cover their heads with the tallith during the more solemn prayers as a sign of reverence before God and as an aid to concentration. In Reform congregations the rabbi, the cantor and the persons called to read the Torah wear the prayer shawl during synagogue services, but it is optional for the members of the congregation. Although women are exempt from the obligation of wearing the tallith, in recent times some women, especially in Reform and Conservative communities, but also in Orthodox congregations, choose to wear it at prayer. It has been customary to bury a male Jew in his tallith.

Rabbi: The word rabbi, which means 'my master', is derived from the Hebrew word *rav*, which means 'great, or 'distinguished'. It seems that the term rabbi began to be used as a title for teachers and sages in Israel only in the first century CE.

The Shekinah is a term used to refer to the Presence of God with his people. The term is derived from the verb *shakan*, 'to dwell', which occurs in such texts as Exod 15:17 (NRSV: 'your abode') and 25:8 which refer to God's dwelling among the Israelites. According to the rabbis, the *Shekinah* dwells, for example, with a husband and wife who live worthy lives, with ten people who pray together, and with a group, or even with an individual, who studies the Torah. These ideas will remind the Christian reader of Jesus' words as recorded by St Matthew (Mt 18:20): 'where two or three are gathered in my name, I am there among them'.

The Shofar is a ritual musical instrument which is made from an animal's horn.

Siddur: the Jewish Prayerbook which contains the prayers and readings that are used in the statutory synagogue services, as well as other material for private devotion.

Skullcap: The skullcap is frequently referred to by its Hebrew name *kippah*. It is also known as a *yarmulka*, a Yiddish word, which may have come from Ukrainian or Polish. There is no biblical injunction which stipulates that men must wear a head covering. Neither does the Talmud contain explicit regulations on this matter. Indeed, covering the head was optional for men in the early centuries of the Common Era as we gather from a Talmud text which states that 'Men sometimes cover their heads and sometimes not; but women's hair is always covered, and children are always bareheaded.' Some Talmud texts show that it was considered an expression of reverence before God to cover the head with the prayer shawl during prayer. The Talmud also records that it was said of a certain rabbi that he would not walk four cubits bareheaded out of reverence for God whom he knew to be always above his head. This example was followed by many Jews, and the practice of wearing a head covering at all times gained acceptance in Jewish communities. From the eighteenth century it became a universal custom. This practice continues in Orthodox communities to this day, and male Orthodox Jews wear at least a skullcap during all their waking hours. Even young Orthodox boys are trained to keep their heads covered as a sign of reverence for God. On Sabbaths and festivals some ultra-Orthodox Jews, mainly in Israel, continue to wear the *shtreimel*, the fur hat that was worn by Polish Jews since the seventeenth century. Conservative Jews usually wear the skullcap at worship, at study and at meals, but they do not consider it obligatory elsewhere. For Reform Jews the wearing of a skullcap is optional even at worship. But in recent times the custom of wearing the *kippah* is becoming more common among them.

Tallith: see above, 'Prayer shawl'.

The Talmud is an extensive commentary on the Mishnah. There are two versions, the Jerusalem Talmud which was completed about the year 400 CE, and the Babylonian Talmud which reached its final stage of development about 500.

Yarmulka: see above 'Skullcap'.

Yeshivah (plural *yeshivot*), literally 'session', an academy for advanced students of Talmud. The traditional *yeshivah* was primarily dedicated to the study of Talmud, and other subjects had little or no place in the curriculum. Until about 1800 *yeshivot* were local establishments with very few students. Shortly after that date they became more organised, and had a structured curriculum and schedule. Many *yeshivot* flourished in Central and Eastern Europe until World War II. Today there are numerous *yeshivot* in different countries, and many of them combine the study of Talmud with a secular education. The Yeshivah University in New York, for example, which is an Orthodox establishment, offers a full programme of academic courses.

Yiddish: the vernacular of most Ashkenazi Jews. It developed from about the year 1100 in the Rhineland and in the Danube valley as an adaptation of the German that was spoken in those areas at that time. It is written in Hebrew characters, and it contains many Hebrew words, especially words that are related to Jewish religious observance. The oldest written evidence, a short inscription in a prayerbook, dates from 1272. After the Crusades, when Jews moved into Eastern Europe, they continued to speak Yiddish, although many Slavic words were incorporated into the language. From about 1800 German Jews began to look down on Yiddish as a debased German, and the language gradually fell into decline in Germany. The vocabulary of the Yiddish that was spoken in Eastern Europe in the period before the Holocaust was about 85 percent German, 10 percent Hebrew, and 5 percent Slavic, with minor contributions from a few other languages. It is estimated that over ten million people spoke Yiddish at that time. Ever since the Nazi decimation of the centres of Yiddish culture, the language is in decline, but a large body of secular and religious Yiddish literature survives. In 1991, it was estimated that about three million people, mainly ultra-Orthodox Jews, spoke Yiddish in such places as the United States, Russia, Israel, etc. Some Universities in Germany now include courses in Yiddish in their German language or Jewish Studies programmes.

Zionism: During the nineteenth century some individuals and groups in Europe were advocating the resettlement of the Jews in Palestine. But it was Theodor Herzl (1860-1904) who, through his writings, by convening the First Zionist Congress in Basel in 1897, and by lobbying influential Jewish figures as well as the political leaders of his day, who brought the issue of a national homeland for the Jews in Palestine on to the international political agenda. There were, however, many Jews who rejected the idea. The American Reform rabbis, for example, in an important document that was published in 1885, and that was to become known as the Pittsburgh Platform, declared that they did not regard the Jews as a nation but as a religious community, and that they did not expect a return to Palestine. Most Orthodox Jews also rejected the Zionist movement, since they believed that the Jews would return to Palestine only in the messianic age, and not as a result of political agitation. The Conservative and Reconstructionist wings of Judaism supported the Zionist ideal, and in the 1930s the Reform movement also rallied to the cause. In 1917 the British Government issued the Balfour Declaration expressing support for a national home for the Jews in Palestine. During the 1920s, 100,000 Jewish immigrants entered Palestine. The Arabs resented the Jewish occupation of what had been their land, and there were continual violent clashes between Jews and Arabs right up to the beginning of World War II. After the Holocaust, practically all Jews saw the need for a Jewish homeland, and when the State of Israel was founded in 1948 they quickly manifested their allegiance to it.

Select Bibliography

Cohn-Sherbok, D., *Judaism. History, Belief and Practice*, London and New York: New York: Routledge, 2003.

de Lange, N., *An Introduction to Judaism*, Cambridge: University Press, 2000.

de Lange, N., and Freud-Kandel (eds), *Modern Judaism*, Oxford: University Press, 2005.

Eisenberg, R. L., *The JPS Guide to Jewish Traditions* (A JPS Desk Reference), Philadelphia: Jewish Publication Society, 2004.

Greenberg, B., *On Women and Judaism. A View from Tradition*, Philadelphia: Jewish Publication Society, 1998.

Heschel, A. J., *The Sabbath: Its Meaning for Modern Man*, New York: Farrar, Strauss and Giroux, 1951.

Keogh, D., *Jews in Twentieth Century Ireland*, Cork: University Press, 1998; reprint 2002.

Küng, H., *Judaism. The Religious Situation of our Time*, London: SCM, 1992.

Neusner, J., *Questions and Answers. Intellectual Foundations of Judaism*, Peabody, Massachusetts: Hendrickson, 2005.

Neusner, J., and Avery-Peck, A. J. (eds), *The Blackwell Companion to Judaism*, Oxford: Blackwell Publishing, and Malden, MA: Blackwell Publishing 2000.

Neusner, J., and Avery-Peck, A. J. (eds), *The Blackwell Reader in Judaism*, Oxford: Blackwell Publishers, and Malden, MA: Blackwell Publishers, 2001.

Robinson, G., *Essential Judaism. A Complete Guide to Beliefs, Customs, and Rituals*, New York and London: Pocket Books, 2000.

Index

The index lists only the more important passages in which a word or term occurs.